A Study of Kiran Desai's The Inheritance of Loss

Chirag Dhandhukiya

Kiran I. Chauhan

CHAPTER - I
INTRODUCTION

Indian Writing in English has contributed in the field of both English fiction and poetry. In the recent years, Indian fiction writers have been widely recognized by the West. Writers like Salman Rushdie, Vikram Seth, Shashi Tharoor, Amitav Ghosh, Arundhati Roy, Kiran Desai have either won the Booker Prize or they have been short listed for other literary prizes. Most of them have been praised for their creative English.

Kiran Desai is one such contemporary writer who got some rare reviews from the literary critics and the writers around the world when her novel ***The Inheritance of Loss*** won the Man Booker Prize for the year 2006. It has been highly praised for its art of story telling and the issues it has raised. Kiran Desai emerged as a new face of Indian English Writing. The book topped chart of the international best sellers for months and Kiran Desai officially stamped her arrival in the Indian English Literary scene.

It was during this time that we came across some good articles and a few interviews and reviews in various magazines, journals and on internet about the book and the author and we felt that a study can be undertaken on the novel to know those unique features which make the novel "an original voice" as described by the Booker Committee. Apart from this, Kiran Desai, being a daughter of the famous Indian English writer Anita Desai, caught our fancy.

Before proceeding with this research, let us know few things about her first novel ***Hullabaloo in the Guava Orchard*** (1998). Her insight and comic sense make the novel 'a must read' for the good mood. The idea of the 'Baba of the tree' delivering sermons is fascinating. The novel is ironical and written in a light vein. But Kiran Desai's observation of human mind is tremendous. She got instant fame when the novel appeared.

So far as her second novel ***The Inheritance of Loss*** is concerned it took almost eight years to take its proper shape. Kiran Desai wrote and rewrote it several times before it was given for publication. So it was clear that she wanted to deliver some substance and not just embellished words. In first reading, it found confusing. The constantly shifting narrative between the Judge and Biju confuses. But at the same time Kiran Desai raises some important issues in the course of the novel. She brilliantly manages her parallel narrative and her linguistic adventures catching our attention. It was thought that a study can be made to link her with her literary ancestors who did the same in their fictions. This study tries to trace that invisible link.

1.1 Kiran Desai: As a Fiction Writer

Kiran Desai was born in Delhi in 1971. She is a daughter of a businessman, and her mother, Anita Desai is a renowned Indian English Fiction writer. Kiran Desai was educated in India, England and United States. She studied creative writing at Columbia University. The influence of her mother can be clearly seen on her writings, as she grew up hearing her talk about books, writings and literature. In one of the interviews she said, "All I ever did was read Jane Austen, the Brontes, Huckleberry Finn".

When on Tuesday, 10th October, 2006, her novel **The Inheritance of Loss** won the prestigious Booker Prize, she became the youngest recipient to win this award. Kiran Desai has only two novels to her credit: **Hullabaloo in the Guava Orchard** (1998) and **The Inheritance of Loss** (2006). Kiran Desai was universally praised for her first novel. She took almost two years to finish her first novel. She thanks her Indian childhood for the novel. The novel is hilarious so far as narrative is concerned. She shows very unconventional method of writing. It is a story of an unemployed town lad Sampath, who is happy doing nothing. But his father made him work, so he leaves the home to a distant guava orchard. He climbs one of the Guava trees and finds solace there. But the fate willed otherwise, he was traced and recognized not as Sampath, but as 'the Baba of the tree'. He was made to preach sermons from his abode until the apes notice him. Desai's tone is ironic as well as comic. She attacks society as well as bureaucracy at large. In her interview to a daily, she says, "It is a comedy and it is satiric in many ways…But I think any one with a sense of humour would enjoy it." The language used is simple and very much a part of our day-to-day life. She writes from her heart and rejects all theories of writing that get told in writing workshops.

But for her second novel ***The Inheritance of Loss*** (2006), she moves from a town to the continents. It has much wider canvass than her first novel. Kiran Desai took almost eight years to complete it. The original book, in her own words, had become a "monster". She wrote 1500 pages and cut it down to 300. The book is modelled on her experiences of staying at her Aunt's Himalayan retreat. Her grandfather was a judge who studied at Cambridge's just like her leading fictional character. The novel moves in split settings between the Himalayas and the basement kitchens of New York. In a frank admission, Kiran Desai says initially "no one wanted it (the book). No one cared." Only 2396 copies of it were sold when it entered the award's long list and the sales zoomed as soon as it won the Booker Prize.

The Inheritance of Loss opens with a teenage girl Sai who is an orphan, living with her Cambridge-educated anglophile grandfather Jemubhai. They live near the Mount Kanchenjunga-in the town Kalimpong on the Indian side of the Himalayas. The name of their house is Cho-Oyu. Jemubhai is a retired judge who spends his time playing chess with himself. His only concern is his beloved dog Mutt. Sai was brought there when her parents died in Russia, and now she has fallen in love with her maths tutor Gyan, who is a Gurkha. Parallel to this in Kalimpong, we are shown the life of Biju, the son of Jemnbhai's cook. Biju is an illegal immigrant in New York who is moving from one job to another.

What binds all these characters together is a common experience of humiliation "certain moves made long ago had produced all of them." Desai writes, referring centuries of oppression by the economic and cultural power of the West.

Almost all Kiran Desai's characters have been shocked by their encounters with the West. As a student, isolated in racist England, the future judge feels" barely human". Yet on his return to India, he finds himself one of them. He deserted his wife for she was not like him, an anglophile.
The judge is one of those "ridiculous Indians" who has nothing but the past to talk about. Sai does not dwell in the past and is glad to be out of the

convent where she used to live when her parents were in Russia. She is happy with Gyan. It was only when Gyan joins the insurgents for their demand for 'Gorkhaland' that the trouble begins in her life. She could not digest Gyan's reality of a poor slum dwelling Nepali.

Meanwhile Biju's life in New York is worst. He is fed up of changing work places. His illegal stay in America also haunts him all the time. The dreams that brought him to America have almost shattered and he wants to go back to India. Back home, the Gorkha movement has gathered momentum and the town of Kalimpong has come to hold. In such a situation, Biju arrives back and gets looted by the hooligans. The novel ends with Biju meeting his father and Gyan's reunion with Sai.

Kiran Desai explores complicated issues as colonialism, racism, terrorism, immigration, love, hate, regret, hope and the myth of both India and America. Though it took her eight years to shape it but it richly fulfills all the criteria of a good work of art. An original story, in a style attempted by only a few Indian writers, Kiran Desai deserves the Booker Prize for such a work. One of the judges Hermione Lee observed while announcing the Man Booker Prize for the year 2006.

> *We are delighted to announce that the winner of the Man booker Prize for 2006 is Kiran Desai's* The Inheritance of Loss, *a magnificent novel of humane breadth and wisdom, comic tenderness and powerful political acuteness. The winner was chosen, after a long, passionate and generous debate, from a shortlist of five other strong and original voices.*

Apart from this, the novel is highly praised for its linguistic experiments and narrative style. Kiran Desai gracefully treads on the path paved by Desani, Rushdie, and Arundhati Roy. Her meticulousness catches our attention. In Gary Shteyngart's words, "If god is in the details, Ms. Desai has written a holy book."

1.2   Indian Writing in English: A Historical Perspective

Indian Writing in English has come quite a long way from the mere use of English language to the authentic tool for expressing one's ideas, thoughts, concepts and imagination. It has attained maturity, but it is not that it suddenly emerged from nowhere. It has had its phases of development. In this chapter, an attempt has been made to trace the history and development of Indian fiction in English.

Indian writers in English have made the most significant contribution to the field of the novel. Ever since the publication of Bankimchandra Chatterjee's **Rajmohan's Wife** in 1864, Indian novel has grown considerably in bulk, variety and maturity. What began as a 'hot-house plant' has now attained a luxuriant growth and branched off in more directions than one. The development of Indian novel follows certain definite patterns, and it is not difficult to trace its gradual progression from the imitative stage to the realistic to psychological to the experimental stage.

With the advent of the thirties the "Big Three" of Indian Writing in English arrived on the scene, and they were the virtual harbinger of true Indo-English novel, though almost all the time they inevitably portrayed the village life and the concomitant effect of freedom movement. They could not keep themselves away from the pulls of the Gandhian philosophy, which consciously or unconsciously entered their creative writing. But it is in this phase that we come across excellent novels for the first time, as is evident from Mulk Raj Anand's **Untouchable** (1935), R.K. Narayan's **Swami and Friends** (1935) and Raja Rao's **Kanthapura** (1938).

It was R.K. Narayan who first portrayed a purely Indian sensibility. He is India's most revered and prolific novelist. In the words of K .R. Srinivas Iyengar,

> *He is one of the few writers in India who take their craft seriously, constantly striving to improve the instrument, pursuing with a sense of dedication what may often seem to be the mirage of technical perfection. There is a norm of excellence below which Narayan cannot possibly lower himself.* (1962: P.359)

Though R.K. Narayan was not so radical as Raja Rao in his appropriation of English, Narayan is part of the process, which in his own word is an 'Indianisation' of English. For Narayan, the language fulfills its purpose by 'conveying unambiguously the thought and acts of a set of personalities'. This highlights one important aspect of post-colonial literature; conveying experience in a language, which is foreign to the writer's cultures.

Mulk Raj Anand showed to the West that there was more in the orient that could be inferred from Omar Khayyam, Tagore or Kipling. When he started writing fiction, he decided that he would prefer the familiar to the fancied. He had first seen his heroes as pieces of trembling humanity and loved them before he sought to put them into his books.

If Mulk Raj Anand could castigate the traditional social set up in his writings, Raja Rao would rise up in to a horizon of his own created by metaphysics. Raja Rao was a child of the Gandhian age, and reveals in his work his sensitive awareness of the forces let loose by the Gandhian revolution as also of the thwarting or steadying pulls of past tradition. But as a user of a foreign language he also confesses his limitation in a 'Forward' given by himself in his first novel **Kanthapura**. He writes,

> *English is the language of our intellectual make up whereas our mother tongue is the language of our emotional make up.* (1938: P.8)

Such was the creative genius of these "Big Three" that they discovered a whole new world in Indo English fiction. They examined minutely the Indian sensibility and exposed the foibles of the Indian way of life.

In the forties, G.V. Desani's **All About H. Hatterr** (1948) made a major breakthrough in formal experimentation and became a masterpiece of remarkable artistry. Hatterr's dazzling, puzzling, leaping prose is the first genius effort to go beyond the Englishness of the English language. It created indelible impression in the minds of the readers by its highly evocative narrative technique and the language unparalleled in the history of Indo- Anglo fiction.

A lawyer by training, Khushwant Singh's most enduring work has been in the field of Sikh history and biography. His novel **Train to Pakistan** (1956) projects with pitiless precision a picture of the bestial horrors enacted on the Indo-Pakistan border region during the days of partition in 1947.

After the 1950's, however, Indian novelists interest moved from the public to private sphere. They began to delineate in their works the individual's quest for the self in all varied complex forms along with his problems. Most of them in their eagerness to find new themes "renounced the larger world in favour of the inner man" and engaged themselves in "a search for the essence of human living".

A concern to discover some notion of 'authentic being' runs through the five novels written by Arun Joshi. A striking feature of Joshi's fiction is his experimentation with different narrative techniques.

Novelists like Anita Desai, Arun Joshi and Nayantara Sahgal changed through their works the face of Indian English novel and their works contain seeds of future development. Anita Desai is one of India's leading authors. Most of Desai's novels reveal the break down of relationship. She deals with the psychological aspects of her characters. Anita Desai explored the inner climate, the climate of sensibility in her novels and added a new dimension to the achievement of Indian women writers in English fiction.

While the trios are still creatively alive, the novelist of second generation keeps on bringing out remarkable novels from time to time. The contribution of Kamala Markandanya, Manohar Malgaonkar and others have already been recognized in and outside India.

Beginning with Ruth Prawer Jhabvala, known for engaging comedies of North Indian Urban middle class life, the women novelists have displayed not only authenticity but also brought a freshness to their works whereas Kamala Markandaya takes us to the heart of a South Indian village where life has apparently not changed for centuries. She depicted rustic and urban realism in her work.

Another writer Nayantara Sahgal, with her work ***Rich Like Us*** (1985), has shown a very charming way of story telling, and Kamala Das with her autobiographical and bold works treaded the paths hitherto unknown for Indo-Anglian novelists.

Among the contemporary writers, Amitav Ghosh has shown his genius in the Indian English fiction. His two novels - ***The Circle of Reason*** (1986) and ***The Shadow Lines*** (1988) established Ghosh as "the finest writer who were born out of the post *Midnight's Children* revolution in Indo-Anglian fiction.

Vikram Seth attained a dizzy height of success with ***The Golden Gate*** (1986) and ***A Suitable Boy*** (1993). He stunned the literary world with his novel ***A Suitable Boy.*** In its forbidding size, the novel can be compared with Leo Tolstoy's ***War and Peace*** or Marcel Proust's ***Remembrance of Things Past.***

Upamanyu Chatterjee, with his novel ***English August*** (1988), got great success. His tone was ironic and he hit all the foibles of the Indian bureaucracy. Chatterjee brilliantly uses Indianised English in the novel. His contemporary Shashi Tharoor's ***The Great Indian Novel*** (1989) is one of the greatest achievements of Indian English fiction. In the 1990s, Rohinton Mistry has emerged as a significant novelist. His ***Such a long Journey*** (1991) is his maiden attempt in the genre in which he deals with the predicament of modern life.

It is perhaps no exaggeration to say that unexpected and overwhelming changes in Western attitudes toward India and Indian Literature came when Salman Rushdie's novel ***Midnight's Children*** was published in 1981. In the novel, Rushdie conjures up a generation of Indians born at midnight 15 August 1947. He writes,

> *What made the event noteworthy... was the nature of these children, every one of the whom was, through some freak of biology or perhaps owing to some preternatural power of the moment, or just conceivably by sheer coincidence... endowed with features, talents or faculties which can only be described as miraculous. It was as though ... history, arriving at a point of the highest*

significance and promise, had chosen to sow, in that instant, the seeds of a future which would genuinely differ from anything the world has seen up to that time. (p.195)

Perhaps the most interesting aspect of the fiction at the turn of the present century, from the Indian point of view, is the emergence of new talent. A number of novelists have produced significant novels, making a mark in the literary world. The most sensational literary event in the recent past was probably, the publication of Salman Rushdie's magnum opus **Midnight's Children** which became an international success instantly on its release. It created generation of young Indian novelists who eagerly followed his footsteps.

What is still more important is these novelist's efforts to reinterpret and rewrite the history of post independence modern India. Besides, these novelists have shown a perceptive understanding of the predicament of the modern man. The novels published in recent years also bear witness to profound changes taking place in Indian society.

Arundhati Roy is one such talented writer of the post- *Midnight's Children* era who shows real psychological depth while conveying the realities of culture and history. Her novel **The God of Small Things** has earned much critical attention all over the world and fetched her the Booker Prize. Undoubtedly, Roy has managed to free her from the shackles of conventional writing. She successfully experimented with the language, and has been duly rewarded for that.

As with Arundhati Roy, Kiran Desai's work also manages to explore the post-colonial chaos and despair. Her first novel **Hullabaloo in the Guava Orchard** satirises society at large. Her novel **The Inheritance of Loss** (2006) spans continents, generations, cultures, religions, and races. She handles all these with ease like a master craftsman. Her narrative style, creative use of language and handling of plot put her among the leading Indian English fiction writers. And this is acknowledged by the Booker Prize she got for the novel and the international acclaim.

Thus, Indian fiction in English has come a long way from the triumvirates of the thirties to the modern recent English fiction writers. The language which was once treated as a language of the foreigner or the language of the elite class is viewed differently. As the number of readers Indian English fiction has increased. So the quality of writing has also improved. The writers are now no longer active users of English but they have English as their first language (Lingua franca). They express themselves with native proficiency. They are the writers who think and write in one language, which is English. They have travelled in various continents and they have something substantial to tell their readers. Indian English fiction is now a world literature. It has struggled, endured indifferences of the west and now finally emerged as a clear winner among the recent fiction writers.

1.3 The Post-Colonial Writing

Recent years have witnessed a good number of Indian English fiction writers who have stunned the literary world with their works. Their works have enriched the world literature, and they have been awarded with accolades and prizes in the field of literature. But a careful study of their development makes it clear that there are two kinds of writers who contributed to the genre of novel: The first group of writers focused on the various social problem of India like poverty, class discrimination, social dogmas, rigid religious norms etc. which has an appeal to the West. The second group of writers includes those who are global Indians, who are Indian by birth but they have lived abroad, so they see Indian realities objectively. They are at ease with the English language and have enriched English language with their creativity. Even though handling Indian sensibility these writers are no longer the slavish imitators of English. They have used English so creatively that the freshness becomes a prominent feature in their language.

They have experimented with the language and fused Indian spirit in the foreign language. They have coined new words and idiomatic expressions in English and added a new flavour in English language. Some of these terms are now accepted as English words. The West relished it with zest and they have their permanent place in the world literature.

These writers are inspired by post-colonial commonwealth writers like Chinua Achebe and Wole Soyinka. These writers have similar experiences as suppressed, and from these they emerge with their creativity to stun the West with their literary genius.

The three most prominent African writers since 1950s are Chinua Achebe and Wole Soyinka from Nigeria and Ngugi Wa Thiong'o from Kenya. Each has responded in different ways to the problems faced by African writers in English. These include the use of English, the representation of Africans and their history, post-independence political corruption and the significance of traditional culture in modern Africa.

Chinua Achebe was the first black African writer in English to gain wide spread critical acclaim from the international English speaking world. His first novel ***Things Fall Apart*** (1958) is regarded as a milestone of African literature. It is predominantly set in Umuofia, an Ibo village in Eastern Nigeria, when the white man first arrives. It tells about the Ibo way of Life. Throughout the novel, Achebe uses original Ibo vocabulary and style of English, sensitive to the rhythm and pace of that language. He uses local proverbs, folk tales and techniques developed by oral storytellers.

Achebe was a conscious artist of the language. In his essay *"The African Writer and the English Language"* (1964), Achebe wrote (Barlow, 2001: P.34) that the African writer should "aim at fashioning out an English which is at once universal and able to carry his peculiar experience... a new English... altered to suit its new African surroundings". This statement clearly suggests Achebes attitude to the use of English what he wanted in the writing was local flavor in the foreign language. Achebe's statement echoes Raja Rao's statement in the "Foreward" to ***Kanthapura***.

Like Achebe, Wole Soyinka is one of the major forces of African literature. He attempted all the major forms of literature, which brought him the Nobel Prize for literature in 1986. Despite a range of European influences on his work, from Samuel Beckett's absurdist ***Waiting for Godot*** (1955) to earlier 17th Century comedy of manners, Soyinka is very much an African dramatist. He uses religious rituals and folk tales of Africa, and amuses his readers with his African English.

It has been argued that post-colonial writing is part of a process whereby native writers reject the English culture, and reassert the indigenous culture to which they belong. Rather than trying to imitate the literature of their colonial masters they go back to their traditions and use the English language with native touch.

The post- colonial writers use the English language as medium of their expression. They have totally replaced the discourse to suit their style of writing. There are two distinct processes by which they do this. The first process is the *abrogation* or denial of the privilege of English. The second, the *appropriation* and reconstruction of the language of the centre (Empire), the process of capturing and remolding the language to new usages become important to them.

Abrogation is a refusal to the categories of the imperial culture, its aesthetic, its illusory standard of correct usage, and its assumptions of a traditional and fixed meaning inscribed in the words. Whereas *appropriation* is the process by which the language is taken and made to bear the burden of one's own cultural experience. As Raja Rao puts it,' to convey in a language that is not one's own, the spirit that is one's own'. So, language is adopted as a tool and utilized in various ways to express widely differing culture experiences. Thus, this literature is therefore always written out of the tension between the abrogation of the received English which speaks from the centre, and the act of appropriation which brings it under the influence of a vernacular tongue.

We can see three main types of linguistic groups within post-colonial discourse: monoglossic, diglossic and polyglossic. Monoglossic groups are those single language societies using English as a native tongue. Diglossic societies are bilingual societies. They have English as the language of government and commerce, and the literary use of English demonstrates variation influenced by the mother tongue. Polyglossic or polydialectal societies have a multitude of dialects interwoven to form a comprehensible linguistic item. This occurs from the reconstruction of the regional English varieties and the varieties which produce national and regional peculiarities.

The English language has that inherent quality to absorb these new elements. In the words of C.D. Narasimhaiah (Barlow, 2001: P.8) "English is not a pure language but a fascinating combination of tongues welded into a fresh unity." The readers often come across words which are culture specific. However such uses of language as untranslatable words have an important function. They signify a certain cultural experience which they can not hope to reproduce. In the foreward to his novel **Kanthapura** Raja Rao explains the particular tasks faced by the writer in conveying cultural specificity in a different language. He writes,

> *The telling has not been easy, one has to convey in a language that is not one's own the spirit that is one's own. One has to convey the various shades and omissions of a certain thought movement that looks maltreated in an alien language. I use the word alien, yet English is not really an alien language to us. It is the language of our intellectual make up like Sanskrit or Persian was before — but not of our emotional make up. We are all instinctively bilingual, many of us writing in our own language and English. We cannot write like the English. We should not. We cannot write only as Indians. (P.VII)*

The use of the English language is often a vital issue when we approach the post colonial texts. The obvious reason is that the native writers were using a medium that was a foreign language and it did not naturally reflect the culture and experiences that they wished to convey, they have had to shape it to suit their purpose often changing of language is seen as their refusal to be dominated by the culture of their earlier masters. Apart from this, the psychological significance lies in the fact that shaping a language to one's own needs shows a confidence, a feeling of ownership. It gives a sense of empowerment to the user. Raja Rao's **Kanthapura** (1938) is a good specimen how he has appropriated English. In the novel, we have something:

> *And then men rush from this street and that street and the police Inspector seeing this hesitates before coming down, and Rachanna barks out again "Mahatma Gandhi Ki Jai" and the police inspector shouts, "Arrest that swine!" and when they come to*

arrest him everybody gets round him and says, "No we'll not give him up." And the police Inspector orders, "Give them a licking, and from this side and that there is the bang of the lathi and men shriek and women weep and the children begin to cry and groan and more and more men go forward towards Moorthy, and more police beat them, and then Moorthy says something to the police Inspector and the police Inspector nods his head, and Moorthy comes along the veranda and say, "Brothers!" and there is such a silence that the Kartik lights glow brighter... for the lights were all out and the leaders all arrested, and as Moorthy is being dragged down the steps Rachanna's wife and Madanna's wife and Sampanna's wife and Papamma and Sankamma and veeramma come forward. (P.178)

The passage shows how the English language is used with native vocabulary. Raja Rao's flow of telling the thing is almost like that of our languages.

The use of foreign words was not new to Indian writing in English. This can be traced far back to the time of trio of the thirties. R.K.Narayan uses words like *pyol* and *jutka*. Raja Rao has *sthalapurana* and *harikatha* in **Kanthapura** (1935). Mulk Raj Anand and Khushwant Singh also used Indian words in their works. And G.V. Desani's **All about H. Hatterr** (1948) is a masterpiece so far as the use of Indian words are concerned he almost made the novel bilingual.

G.V.Desani is also one of the early writers of Indian English fiction who experimented with the English language. He gave native sensibility to the language. His novel **All About H. Hatterr** (1948) is widely praised for his linguistic experiments. T.S.Eliot goes up to saying, "In all my experience, I have not met with anything like it." He has shown a very unusual way of story telling in this novel. He begins the novel with a foreward by himself:

London, October 23, 1945
WHEREFORE during '39 – '45, these warring years, an appalling thing happened to me. I acquired a major fault. I became secretive, told lies, at any rate, rarely the whole truth. Life seemed

> so many clashes and contests, sorry! And, well, invention helps.
> (P.9)

Apart from this, Desani coined new terms in English. The terms which are near to our heart as Indians, like 'sky – speech', for *'akaashwani'*; 'space and sky clothed' for *'digambara'*, 'an eight limbed reverence' for *'sashtang'* etc. One of the reviewers observes, "Desani's verbal invention is indefatigable,his linguistic sources inexhaustible." At the same time a large number of Indian words are used as, *'Hindustaaniwalla', 'Salaam', 'Dhobin', Sahib, 'Todii', Kismet, Topi, Jaldi, Dharna, Panchyat, Shikar, Chakras, Nirvana, attar, sthula, sukshama, parmeshvara, Nagas* etc. This shows that Desani is consciously fusing these terms with the English language. He created a masterpiece with his this quality. About his writing, he says,

> *I write rigmarole English, staining your goodly godly tongue, may be: but, friend, I forsook my Form, School and Head, while you stuck to yours, learning reading, 'riting and 'rithmatic.*

In Desani's writing, we can feel that urge which made him write his novel in such a style. A feeling that the English is not the private property of the English, even we can, the people of the other world, write with ease, is seen every where. The narrative has that touch of 'Sanskrit' classics as:

> *Well, Mr. H. Hatterr, said my pal, 'as an Indian, and a Hindu student gentlemen, I am deeply attached to the ancient classics. According to the sages, all women can be summed up and recognized under four species. In other words, the Lotus, the Art, the Sea – Shell, and the Elephant. These are the four sorts of woman. The Lotus- woman is A1 vintage.* (P.42)

Such a use of language by an Indian was something rare when the native English writers reigned the literary scenario. In Desani own words, "a language deliberately designed to mystify the majority, tempt 'em to start guessing, and interpreting our real drift, and allegory, what the hell we mean…" Anthony Burgess in his introduction to **All About H. Hatterr** remarks:

> *It is the language that makes the book, a sort of creative chaos that grumbles at the banks. It is what may be termed Whole Language, in which philosophical terms, the colloquialisms of Calcutta and London, Shakespearian archaisms, bazaar whinings, quack spiels, references to the Hindu pantheon, the jargon of Indian litigation, and Shrill babu irritability seeth together.*

After Desani, Rushdie was the major Indian English writer who experimented with the language. He was highly praised for his creative use of language in his magnum opus **Midnights children** (1981). The novel got the Booker Prize in the year 1981. It attempts adventurously in the narrative style and what could be done with Indian material in the English language in particular. Rushdie almost takes a linguistic risk with the abundant use of street language of the cities, daring to translate idioms and metaphors and occasional bilingual puns. But we cannot deny the fact that there is a generation of Indians for whom English is like their day to day language. They are at ease with it and therefore, capable of using it in playful, creative and impure ways, mixed with other Indian languages. We often come across such mixed English at various informal places but to write a novel with this is quite bizarre but Rushdie ventured and he conquered.

In the novel, Rushdie showed the attitude as he himself claimed 'the empire writing back' with a vengeance. He writes

> *Those of us who do use English do so in spite of our ambiguity towards, it, or perhaps because of that perhaps because we can find in that linguistic struggle a reflection of other struggles taking place in the real word.... To conquer English may be to complete the process of making ourselves free."* (Mukherjee, 1999 : P.71)

We can see a typical post-colonial attitude in his writings. Having been taught the masters language, one may "know how to curse" (The master?) in it, as famously did Caliban in what has now become a post- colonial tenet (sutra).

Rushdie's claim to "conquer English" had a more strictly textual and stylistic dimension. He uses Hindi – Urdu / Hindustan words, phrases and collocations. Rushdie's use of an English nastily flavoured with Hindi begins on the every first page of the novel, where Salim tells us that he has been called by various names, including piece of the moon – 'Chand ka tukra'. Such Indian words, phrases and allusions are everywhere in the novel. There are names of places like Dadar, the Vindhyas, Amul Dairy etc. a list of words from the Indian langauegs as *baap re baap, bhangis, charas and falooda*, words related to religion like *Al-lah, Atharva Veda, Gandharva, Kaliu Yuga* and *Mujahideen* etc. These words are not explained any where in the text, so the readers except Indian readers are left to the mercy of god to interpret them.

After Rushdie's **Midnight's children** in eighties, there was no major contribution in the field of novel from the point of view of linguistic experiments. Somehow the next generation of writers could not reach that height of Rushdie in their style. It was only in the later half the nineties when Arundhati Roy shook the literary world with her style of writing with her first novel **The God of Small Things**. The novel won the Booker prize for 1997. The novel is a good example of how the Indian writers use the English language. Arundhati Roy uses the English language with native ease, and also creates new idioms.

Arundhati Roy's writing is almost unconventional. Her narrative structure makes ample use of past present technique. She also coins new words and uses the local language now and then her style and her choice of words leaves the reader spell bound. (But often the narrative confuses the readers with its complexity). One of the reviewer wrote, "Roy stretches the English language in all directions." The Booker committee praised it with these words, "With extraordinary linguistic inventiveness Roy funnels the history of South India through the eyes of seven years old twins."

So the reason why the judges chose Arundhati Roy's **The God of Small Things** for the Booker prize is very clear. Arundhati Roy has twisted the language to suit her own storytelling. She triumphed because, unlike the others, she had the guts and the overwhelming talent to invert a new idiom and vocabulary to tell the story of a seemingly remote people.

These are the major writers who have shown courage to go beyond the convention in their writings. They tried to break the stereotype of the English fiction. In their attempt of Indianising English they were often criticized for spoiling the English language. But they have created their niche in the Indian English fiction, and their initiative has inspired number of modern Indian English fiction writers to do so.

1.4 Experimentation in English Language by Indian Writers

Indian English fiction writers have often shown their creative genius in their writings. They no longer consider it a foreign language. It is the language in which they can effectively express themselves creatively with native ease. These writers are inspired by the African writers like Chinua Achebe and Wole Soyinka, who successfully fused African spirit in their writings. Often this tendency has made their work difficult for the foreign readers. In the same manner the use of jargons and allusions to Indian myths, legends confuse them. But it was not that they are not aware of it. The indian English fiction writers have created a niche for themselves. Their experiments have caught the attention of the Western scholars and readers. They have also been nominated for the leading international prizes and awards.

In the recent years, some of our Indian writers have been among the Booker Prize winners, which is one of the leading literary prizes after the Nobel Prize for literature. The Booker committee analyses the short listed novels from various angles and chooses the best among them. The novel has to be at par with the world literary standards, it should be original, a well crafted piece of literature from various literary point of view. The Booker Prize comprises a citation and a cheque of £ 50,000. It is doubtless that it also increases the sales of winner's book and it gives international recognition to its writer.

There was a time when the West used to recognize the 'Third World' writers with a sense obligation rather than genuine acceptance. It is often argued that if one wants to be noticed in the west, one should present the East in unfavourable light. Often the Indian writers who present India, its culture in the unfavorable light are considered for the awards. The west has a typical notion about the third world, where their eyes only see poverty, wretchedness, terrorism, lack of system, failure of democracy and so forth. And the writers, voicing one of these are sure to be recognized by the West. But in the last few years, the scenario has changed. The Indian writers are major contributors to the English fiction and they are no longer a 'sympathy seekers'. They have their English and their genuine experience to share.

Apart from this, yet another reason for which Indian writers are also recognized is their innovative experiments in the genre. These writers, who have created a new form, have been handsomely rewarded. It can be a narrative innovation or linguistic experimentation. Such writers have native-like proficiency of the English language, they know how to handle English creatively. So for them form and style are equally important in their story. Often we find autobiographical elements in their works. These writers have reached the height from where they can tell their own tale in the language suitable for their native set. Such writers are often awarded. The Booker Prize for their linguistic experimentation and genuine tale.

If we go back to the list of Indian Booker Prize Winners, we see that the writers of the Indian origin like Salman Rushdie, Arundhati Roy and the recent winner Kiran Desai have one thing common in their writings – they are not traditional Indian English writers. All the three are at ease with the English language, rather English is their first language. So medium is not at all a problem for them. They can use English as naturally as they breathe. And what is more important is that these writers have lived abroad for major part of their life, so they have imbibed and assimilated the Western trends and it lends them the distance to have an objective view on India and Indians. These writers have come across many Englishes of the world and showed the world their English unhesitantly.

In the eighties, Salman Rushdie's ***Midnight's Children*** (1980) attracted the world's attention both by its language and the narrative mode. It has been seen as the quintessential fictional embodiment of the postmodern celebration of decentring and hybridity. It's a good specimen of what could be done with Indian material in the English language. Rushdie almost took linguistic risks by using street language, translated idioms and metaphors to create bilingual puns. We see devices like code-mixing, code-switching and he has also coined new words. In a typical line like "Godown, gudam, warehouse, call it what you like", we have Indian English followed by Hindi followed by proper English. Rushdie himself admits in an interview:

> *The English language is, I think, less of a problem than people make it out to be. But, I think, what happened is that there is a, kind of generation of writers,- I mean I am not [that much] younger than all these writers we are talking about- and I think, that there was that generation, who were basically just about adult at the time of independence, who were very heavily influenced by the English, the classical English, writing. And I think that was their formation, and I think that their instinct was to write in that way. But I think also that by now English is very domesticated in India. (Mukherjee: p.223)*

Rushdie's **Midnight's Children** tracks the pre-colonial, colonial but mostly post-independence life of India through a narrator and protagonist, Saleem Sinai, who was born at the moment of India's formal Independence from Britain. Salim is a versatile story teller, writing his own and nations life and times in a variety of registers. "There are as many versions of India," says Saleem, "as Indians".

One of the legacies of **Midnight's Children** is a vibrant model for rewriting English in dialogue with the Indian regional languages. Anita Desai has claimed that it was only after 'Salman Rushdie came along, that Indian writers finally felt capable of using the spoken language, spoken English, the way it's spoken on Indian streets by ordinary people'. Thus, Rushdie treaded on a different path and was rewarded for that.

Similarly, Arundhati Roy's 1997 Booker Prize Winning Novel **The God of Small Things** shows that novelty of style, which was introduced by Rushdie. It is an autobiographical type of novel. The story resembles Arundhati Roy's personal life in many ways. In the novel, Arundhati Roy is "trying to make the connection between the very smallest of things and the very biggest of things", that makes her the first Indian citizen to win the Booker Prize.

The reason why the judges chose Arundhati Roy's **The God of Small Things** for the Booker Prize is very clear. It was not chosen for its Indian setting or a cross caste erotic love between a Paravan and a Syrian Christian. It was, rather, her verbal exuberance that worked in her favour. For the Booker Prize, it needed a writer of Roy's stature that imparts humour and pathos with ease in a language hitherto used. She twisted the language to suit her own story telling. Rosemary Dinnage wrote in the New York Review of books, "Roy stretches the English language in all directions". The Booker committee also praised the novel.

Arundhati Roy appropriates the English language by bringing it under the influence of the vernacular. She defamiliarizes the language by making it carry the burden of her culture. She often deliberately uses untranslatable words in the novel. It is this aspect of her novel that makes it unconventional and a worthy of our praise.

After Arundhati Roy, Kiran Desai has become the youngest woman writer to win the Booker Prize for her second novel **The Inheritance of Loss** (2006). The novel has received a rare review for its narrative style and its linguistic experiments. Kiran Desai uses bilingual words as well as pure Hindi words in her novel. The tale shuttles between New York and Kalimpong, and Kiran Desai brilliantly portrays both the worlds with ease. Her words beautifully portray richness of Kanchanjenga valley with minute observation of the nature around and at the same her pen becomes razor edged describing the New York life. She brilliantly changes her vocabulary to suit her narration.

Kiran Desai treaded the same path as her literary ancestors like Salman Rushdie and Arundhati Roy. And it is not surprising, that she has been rewarded in the same way. Her novel fulfills all the criteria of a good novel. It travels through cultures, continents, sensibilities and languages. She has successfully appropriated the English language to match style.

Tracing the history of the Indian English Fiction, we can infer that it has developed in various phases. The arrival of the 'trio of thirties' can be considered a unique event in its development. The pre-independence fictions are largely based on freedom struggle and Gandhian ideals. But it has contributed well to the Indianization process of the English language. Writers like Mulk Raj Anand, Raja Rao and R.K. Narayan had their definite stance over the use of the English language with native touch in it. They were the first main stream Indian English writers who literally inaugurated the movement of Indianizing English Language.

Raja Rao undoubtedly takes the credit of formally declaring that aspect of writing fiction in the English language. His **Kanthapura** (1935) is best known for its classic Foreward, which reads very much like a manifesto for the practice of Indian writing in English. The Foreward begins by describing the difficulty of bridging the cultural and historical gap between the English language and the Indian tale. One has to describe in a language that is not one's own the spirit that is one's own. This dichotomy, Raja Rao claims, can only be resolved through a systematic indigenization of English by infusing it with the breathless and unpunctuated 'tempo of Indian life'. So also, faced with the indisputably, Western origins of the novel form, the Indian writer is required to undertake the rather more difficult task of generic appropriation, by relocating the epic within the epic tradition of the **Ramayana** and **Mahabharata.**

It was G.V.Desani who twisted the English language like anything. His **All About H.Hatterr** (1948), for the first time, made a conscious effort to Indianize the English language. The novel is more a sort of Joycean linguistic burlesque where, Indian English much like Joyce's Irish English, relentlessly jostles against all the known rules of grammar and diction. Shakespeare combines with Indian legalese, Anglo Indian rules up against the pompous colonial club talk, and chaos of unpunctuated sentences and arbitrary capitalization but Desani admits," a language deliberately designed to mystify the majority, tempt 'em to start guessing and interpreting our real drift, and allegory, what the hell we mean…"(*All About H.Hatter:1948. P.120*)

Desani's intensely self conscious novel prefigures more recent look like Salman Rushdie's **Midnight's Children** (1981). Its linguistic experimentation and irreverent handling of the great books of the Europe witnessed a second coming for the Indian novel in English. Its messiah was undoubtedly Salman Rushdie. The appearance of **Midnight's Children** in 1981 brought about a renaissance in Indian writing in English. Rushdie showed the courage to paint the English language with Indian colours. He almost wrote bilingual novel with no apology, no footnote and no glossary. The English readers were left to the mercy of god for understanding and interpreting Indian terms. The novel is also innovative from the point of view of the narrative style. Arundhati Roy's debut novel **The God of small Things** also demands our attention in this line. She also successfully experimented with the genre and gave linguistic treat to the readers.

So if we trace this development, we can surely pick up a thread that binds Kiran Desai with other Indian English Fiction writers. That thread is of creative use of language where the writer is using bilingual terms to give his or her work a native touch. Desai is a part of that long tradition of the writers who dare to do something new, something hitherto not much attempted. Her novel shows enough evidence that can put in the tradition of Desani, Rushdie and Arundhati Roy. All these writers have several common things in their writings. They all have shown their genius in their not so traditional narrative. They sometimes baffle the readers with their way of handling their narrative. But what is noteworthy is their creative use of language. They use devices like code mixing, code switching, coining new words, phrases etc. to enchant their readers with linguistic hotch – potch.

The Inheritance of Loss with these aspects fascinates the readers. The novel, though, appears as a simple story of Jemubhai, Sai and Biju but if we carefully analyse it, we notice that it has more things than a simple story of love, hate and hope. Any good reader would feel that touch of a master craftsman in the novel. She took almost eight years in completing this and the book shows the genius of the writer. The study will attempt to find out those aspects of the novel that place it among the tradition of those innovative Indians who made the difference with their exceptionally Indianized fictions. Kiran Desai tries to capture some of the contemporary issues which shake the world. She tries to present a divided world. The movement for the Gorkhaland in the novel is the inevitable outcome of the new world order. At the same time, she focuses on the adverse effect of globalization and how the West lures the East. Everybody wants to go to America to become a 'suited-booted' person. Here the problem of illegal immigrants comes. Desai meticulously harmonizes all these varied things in her not-so-regular narrative.

CHAPTER - II
KIRAN DESAI'S
THE INHERITANCE OF LOSS

Kiran Desai's ***The Inheritance of Loss*** is a tale of a few powerless individuals who are victims of the circumstances. Kiran Desai portrays a complex world where life is almost like a puzzle. Her characters are all puppets controlled by outside situations. She discusses some of the contemporary international issues like globalisation, multiculturalism, economic inequality, fundamentalism and terrorist violence. The novel has a vast canvass. It spans continents, generations, cultures, religions and races.

Like Kiran Desai's first novel- ***Hullaballoo in the Guava Orchard*** (1998), ***The Inheritance of Loss's*** primary setting is India. The remote province of Kalimpong, at the foot-hill of Kanchenjunga in the mid-1980s. The novel begins with the description of the landscape which is central for the events that unfolds.

> *All day, the colours had been those of dusk, mist moving like a water creature across the great flanks of mountains possessed of ocean shadows and depths. Briefly visible above the vapour, Kanchenjunga was a far peak whittled out of ice, gathering the last of the light, a plume of snow blown high by the storms at its summit.* (P.1)

Here in the foothills of Himalayas, "where India blurs into Bhutan and Sikkim" sixteen year old Sai lives with her grandfather – a retired judge named Jemubhai Potatlal Patel, his cook and Mutt his dog. Sai is in love with her mathematics tutor Gyan – a Nepali. Desai at the same time introduces to us Biju – the cook's son who is in New York. Biju is an illegal immigrant in USA hiding himself from the clutches of the authority. These are major characters around whom the novel moves. Their struggle physical or mental makes the novel move ahead. Apart from these, we have minor characters like Uncle Potty, Father Booty, Nani, Lolita, Saeed Saeed etc. who are more types than individuals.

The novel shuttles between Kalimpong and New York. Desai artistically alternates them time and again. She also moves backward and forward while narrating the story of Jemubhai - the Judge. His present status as a loner in Kalimpong and his past life in Cambridge and India, is presented with utmost precision.

In the present, the story is about the events that unfold in February 1986. The judge is living a peaceful life in Kalimpong with his grand-daughter Sai, his beloved dog Mutt and his cook. The loss of the past glory has made the judge a loner. His only interest is in playing chess and that too with himself only. The only living creature to command his attention is Mutt. The valley is disturbed by the Gorkhaland movement. Such thing never touches the judge except for one day when his house – Cho-Oyu has strange visitors. They are young fighters of the movement, badly in need of weapons and donation. They humiliate the judge and loot the house. Desai writes,

> *Both Sai and the cook had averted their gaze from the judge and his humiliation… It was an awful thing, the downing of a proud man. He might kill the witness.* (P.8)

The way Kiran Desai introduces to us various characters in the first chapter is really interesting for instance "Sai, sitting on the Veranda, was reading article about giant squid in an old *National Geographic*.... The judge sat at the far corner with his chessboard, playing against himself". Desai sharply uses one particular thing to tell us about the nature of that character like 'Sai reading National Geographic shows her convent spirit whereas the judge playing chess with himself shows his aloof nature Desai introduces all the major characters and also gives us hints about the events that will follow. She ends the first chapter with these lines.

> *In Kalimpong, high in the northeastern Himalayas where they lived – the retired judge and his cook, Sai and Mutt- there was a report of new dissatisfaction in the hills, gathering insurgency, men and guns. It was the Indian – Nepalese this time, fed up with being treated like the minority in a place where they were the majority. They wanted their own country, or at least their own state, in which to manage their own affairs. Here, where India*

> *blurred into Bhutan and Sikkim, and the army did pull ups and push ups, maintaining their tanks with Khaki paint in case the Chinese grew hungry for more territory than Tibet, it had always been messy map. The papers sounded resigned. A great amount of warring, betraying, bartering had occurred, between Nepal, England, Tibet, India, Sikkim, Bhuta; Darjeeling stolen from here, Kalimpong plucked from there – despite, ah, despite mist charging down like a dragon, dissolving, undoing, making ridiculous the drawing of borders.* (P.9)

This last passage of the first chapter tells us many things about the ongoing events of the world. Desai begins with the situation in Kalimpong but enlarges the problems upto the world level. As an author, she is conscious of various issues. The passage is almost like a commentary on various issues. Ending the first chapter like this, she wants to stress her central idea of the novel. So, it's a kind of an introductory chapter.

The chapter that follows alternates between Jemubhai – the judge, his grand-daughter Sai and the struggle of Biju- the cook's son. The narrative constantly shifts between them. The novelist often comments on the events ironically. It is particularly seen in the narrative of Biju. Biju is the only son of Jemubhai's cook. The cook works hard for him. He even sells illicit liquor to save money for Biju. His *chhang* also fetches him some extra money. He sent Biju to U.S.A as an illegal immigrant. For the cook, Biju is happy there, living a prosperous life. He is fond of telling others about his son's job and his life there.

Contrary to Biju's expectations and the cook's dreams, the new place absolutely rejects Biju. He is always on the run. As an illegal immigrant, it is difficult for him to get a good job and he is not a skilled labour. He can only cook. So, he has to move from one restaurant to another. The wages are meager and the work place is almost a pit of dungeon where there are more people like Biju from various parts of the world. Asians, Africans, Latin Americans all for job. Biju is almost lost in that multicultural world.

Desai shows their plight with utmost sincerity. The dreams that drag them to America soon leave them in a world of chaos. They are exploited everywhere. The constant fear of police and immigrant authority haunts them. They don't have any social life. In fact they don't live there, they just survive. Their occasional visit to the Washington Heights is there only pleasure.

But Biju has adapted himself to the new situation. He has also made good friends there – all are illegal immigrants. So, with common problems, they belong to the same class, the class of slaves.

Kiran Desai's description of the situation there is really eye opener. The adverse effect of globalisation has been vividly portrayed. She writes,

> *Former slaves and natives Eskimos and Hiroshima people, Amazonian Indians and Chiapas Indians and Chilean Indians… World Bank, UN, IMF, everything run by white people. Every day in the paper another thing!.* (P.133)

But there are people like Saeed Saeed who can mould themselves according to the situation. Saeed Saeed is from Zanzibar, living like Biju. They met each other in a kitchen of a restaurant and instantly bonded. Saeed Saeed is a practical man of the world. Biju admires him lot for his tactfulness. It is through his character that Desai shows us the skills required for survival in this mad rush of America. It is not a place for the people like Biju. Biju is almost trapped. He cannot live and at the same time he cannot leave. He is just at the mercy of his fate.

One the one hand, Kiran Desai shows pitiable conditions of the illegal immigrants in America and on the other hand we have a tender love story of Sai. The judge's grand-daughter Sai's love affair with her Nepali maths teacher Gyan is vital part of the novel. Sai represents a class which is totally unaware of the problems of the third world. They speak English and prefer socializing occasionally to have goody goody talk with each other little meaning. Her relationship with Gyan, for the first time puts her before those problems which are never part of her world. Her love to Gyan is a typical teenage love where social consideration is very remote thing. But Gyans active involvement in the movement, his support to the GNLF activist makes her bewilder. For sai, Gyans decision to join them is thoughtless one. She doesn't feel the urge which has overtaken the Gyan's mind. So, the tension between two classes arises. Sai is almost disappointed by Gyan's decision but for Gyan he has sacrificed something for the greater cause.

Kiran Desai, in fact, shows us how the lovers are trapped in the events happening in their town. The insurgency in the valley has shaken the peace. One cannot expect to be untouched by it. It strikes worst when one is innocent or ignorant about them. The same thing happens in the case of Sai. Besides it, Jemubhai's attitude towards her, makes her more miserable for Jemubhai, Sai is a liability. He is just doing his duty.

Besides this, we have stories of Uncle Booty, Noni, Lola etc. but they are less significant to the overall development of the novel. Perhaps the only active character in the novel whose story is eventful is Biju. Biju is almost a picaresque hero moving form one place to another. In his physical journey he also moves from innocence to experienced state. He learns that all that glitters is not gold. His realization of the losses he has had in America is significant. Suddenly he craves for home, his father and he wants to return. Though, Biju got looted in his way back to Kalimpong, his reunion with his father sooths him and he breaks into tears.

Desai ends the novel with an optimistic note where Gyan meets Sai and Biju is back home, to be with his father. It is perhaps the most touching event. Desai ends the novel as follows:

> *Pitaji ?" said the figure, all ruffles and colors.*
> *Kanchenjunga appeared above the parting clouds, as it did only very early in the morning during this season.*
> *"Biju ?" whispered the cook*
> *"Biju !" he yelled, demented*
> *Sai looked out and saw two figures leaping at each other as the gate swung open.*
> *The five peaks of Kanchenjunga turned golden with the kind of luminous light that made you feel, if briefly, that truth was apparent.*
> *All you needed to do was to reach out and pluck it.* (P.324)

Kiran Desai is a confident and talented writer. Her novel shows this wisdom. It is both funny and bitterly sad, but generally optimistic. Desai's scope is broad and she looks at the consequences of large cultural and political forces.

But this is not the only thing that makes her novel different. Desai's unconventional narrative, which constantly moves backward and forward, is also interesting. The constant shuttling between the judge's story and Biju's eventful life keep the readers baffled. But her linguistic liberty enchants them at the same time. Her language makes the novel all the more interesting. Following her literary ancestors like Desani and Rushdie, Kiran Desai beautifully moulds her novel into Indian spirit. She attracts the readers' attention with her unusual narrative and linguistic experiments.

CHAPTER - III
A CRITICAL ANALYSIS OF THE NOVEL

3.1 Thematic Concerns

Kiran Desai's ***The Inheritance of Loss*** touches some very sensitive issues of the world. Basically it's a 'Globalised novel for a globalised world'. It voices the class of marginalized and the class who has lost their identity in the multicultural society. These are typical post- modern elements. The novel presents the struggle of the minority to gain identity and recognition. Identity or loss of Identity is perhaps the single most dominating factor that one can feel in the novel. Major characters have created their illusionary world only to avoid their inevitable fate which haunts them all.

The novel bounces between an insurgency in India and the immigrants experience in New York. Both the aspects have one thing common, they are about their place, their land where they can live with peace and they will have their identity. They don't feel a sense of belongingness to sooth their soul. Desai aptly quotes Jorge Luis Borges in the beginning of the novel,

> *They speak of humanity.*
> *My humanity is in feeling we are all*
> *Voices of the same poverty*
> *They speak of homeland*
> *My homeland is the rhythm of a guitar… (p.-I)*

Desai, from the very first chapter, introduces us to the problem of 'homeland'. The creation of ghettos is a major concern of the world, people are divided in the name of race and religion, and the problem of superior race religion and inferior race religion arises. This problem has swept all the corners of the world. The reason for this may be practical that we feel safe among our people and in our land but the outcome of this is terrifying. The geographical boundaries have created psychological divisions. And these divisions will strikes on you today or tomorrow irrespective of the corner you choose to hide yourself in solitude. As Desai puts,

> *In Kalimpong, high in the north east Himalayas where they lived – retired judge and his cook, Sai, and Mutt – there was a report of new dissatisfaction in the hills, gathering insurgency, men and guns. It was the Indian – Nepalese this time, fed up with being treated like the minority in a place where they were the majority. They wanted their own country, or at least their own state, in which to manage their own affairs. Here, where India blurred in Bhutan and Sikkim, and the army did pull – ups and push-ups, maintaining their tanks with khaki paint in case the Chinese grew hungry for more territory than Tibet, it had always been a messy map. The papers sounded resigned. A great amount of warning, betraying, battering had occurred, between Nepal, England, Tibet, India, Sikkim, Bhutan, Darjeeling stolen from here, Kalimpong plucked from there despite, oh, despite the mist charging down like a dragon, dissolving, undoing, making, ridiculous the drawing of boarders.* (P.9)

Here, we see typical 'minority-majority' problem. They feel that they have been deprived of their rights because they are minority. The class, which was oppressed for centuries, is asserting itself. The struggle for control over the other has got momentum. This control can be economic, political or cultural. The inevitable outcome of this is geographical imbalance. The native becomes refugee overnight and the rest is a story of 'homeland' and blood – bath. This is echoed in the refrain:

> "Jai Gorkha",
> "Gorkhaland for Gorkhas".

The homeland movements are getting momentum everywhere. And the guerrilla war has swept half of the world. Struggle for Nagaland for the Nagas, Khalistan for the Sikhs, Bodoland for the Bodo tribe, Sindh for the Sindhis and so on. It seems that there is no end, to this as they call themselves 'liberation movements'. Young minds are brain washed to join them and they have been used as the scapegoats. Desai writes," Then one day fifty boys, members of the youth wing of the GNLF, gathered to swear an oath at Mahakaldara to fight to the death for the formation of a homeland, gorkhaland…. While suddenly, everyone was using the word insurgency."

The novel presents a post-colonial chaos. The system is on the verge of collapsing or has collapsed. People who were ruled by the empire are now free only to be ruled by others. It is as if the oppressor changed the oppressed are the same. But now they want to rebel against the forces that had tortured them. They feel,

> *"It is better to die than live as slaves",*
> *"We are constitutionally tortured".* (P.126)

In the novel, Gyan is one such person who represents the rebels. He feels that stir within and he is prepared to fight. His rebellion spirit is put in the following words,

> *and once again he [Gyan] felt the stir of purity. He would have to sacrifice silly kisses for his adulthood. A feeling of martyrdom crept over him, and with purity for a cause came ever more acute worries of pollution. He was sullied by the romance...* (P.175)

As with Gyan, Biju is one such person who craves for permanent place. He is an illegal immigrant in New York. His struggle to get the 'green card' shows the third world's mad rush for the west. People feel that it is the land where dreams come true. Such misconception tempts many illegal immigrants there. Desai, who resides in New York, must have a first hand experience of their plight. Far from their home and family, they struggle to survive. They work here and there, and live almost like beggars. Biju's condition is no better as Desai observes,

Biju at the Baby Bristo
Above, the restaurant was French, but below in the kitchen it was Mexican and Indian. And when a Paki was hired, it was Mexican, Indian, Pakistan.

Biju at Le Colonial for the authentic colonial experience.
On top, rich colonial, and down below, poor native. Colombian, Tunisian, Ecuadorian, Gambian.

> *On to the Stars and Stripes Diner. All American flag on top, all Guatemalan flag below. Plus one Indian flag when Biju arrived.* (P.21)

Desai highlights how the west lures the third world. We have created stories of the western world. For us it is a land where one can make a fortune. It has been called the land of opportunities but the fact is altogether different. Our encounter with the West is one-sided where we are introduced to its technological advancements, economic freedom and multicultural society. People like Biju get tempted by it. He can see the other, less known, side of that society when he reaches there.

Kiran Desai lives in New York and she is part of that multicultural society so she can write about it with ease. She must have seen hundreds of Bijus there whose dreams are butchered in that city. She shows how Asians are treated there. They are a class of labour to work for them. And now they want to make them their consumers. By the virtue of being billions in number the Asians will provide them the market to sell their any rubbish thing. Desai writes,

> *"We need to get aggressive about Asia", the businessmen said to each other. "Its opening up, new frontier, millions of potential consumers, being buying power in the middle classes, china, India, potential for cigarettes, diapers, Kentucky fried, life insurance, water management, cell phones- big family people, always on the phone, all those men calling their mothers, all those mothers calling all their many, many children's this country is done, Europe done, Latin America done, Africa is a basket case except for oil, Asia is the next frontier. Is there oil anywhere there?"* (P.136)

Desai voices some of the recent concerns of the third world. The West is the single biggest consumer of oil but they no longer want to buy it from the third world. Why should one buy the thing which one can easily snatch from other? The recent political development in the Middle East and Asia is a good example of it.

Globalisation has an adverse effect on the third world. A small group of population lives in affluence, unaware of the world outside. The world which follows the tenet of the survival of the fittest. Desai introduces such people in a very subtle way. Lola, Noni, Uncle Potty belong to this class. They wear Marks and Spencer underwear, eat tin-packed food, read Jane Austen and National Geographic and talk about their experiences in England, only to curse India. For them "India is a sinking ship'.

The novel vividly portrays colonized mindset. Jemubhai-the judge is a good example of this. Born in a rich Patel family of Gujarat, Jemubhai prepares to go to England for ICS. It seems that the Patels have a fascination for foreign country. Jemubhai almost becomes a prized possession for the family. But Jemubhai's encounter with the other world is shocking. He becomes a victim of racial discrimination. The first thing, he was made to feel, was that he was not one of them. He was a brown among them a natural ugly to be precise. He was humiliated like, "Phew, he stinks of curry!" Desai vehemently condemns on the racism of the west. Jemubhai receives a cultural shock in England and the attitude of the people makes him feel barely human.

Kiran Desai ironically presents Jemubhai's past experience as an Indian in England when he poses himself as an anglophile. The judge now sips beef tea and reads "How to Speak Hindustani" since he is a *pucca* English. Jemubhai's reunion with his old friend Bose proved to be disastrous, as some old wounds get opened. Jemubhai had the worst time in the racist England. Bose's words show the contempt they had for those Goras. He says,

> *Goras – get away with everything don't they? Bloody white people. They are responsible for all the crimes of the century!* (P.206)

Desai juxtaposes the situation in a very subtle way. The Jemubhai, who had the worst English experience, pretends to be English. Perhaps, it makes him a person with distinction in India.

Jemubhai's past experience has made him bitter. His behaviour with his wife is quite disgusting. The judge feels ashamed of her. He believes that she should not go out of the house. Nimi almost becomes his headache. The judge feels that his wife will mar his reputation in the society with her behaviour and so he sends her away to her parents' home for the rest of her life. The judge becomes a loner and perhaps this is the reason why he chose Kalimpong for his retired life.

Kiran Desai shows how various characters are struggling for the single goal of identity it can be for establishing one's identity. It can be for lost identity or it can be for want of it. Even the Gorkhas struggle for their homeland is basically for their identity. We feel that we must have our own place; we should belong to certain class or society. It gives us a sense of fulfillment. We feel protected.

Biju's struggle as an illegal immigrant in New York has been given an ironic touch, by Kiran Desai. Biju, who was "the luckiest boy in the whole world", is struggling for the survival. Desai gives us the moving account of those ruined lives. She observes, "They would never know how many of them went astray". The green card struggle is eternal for those. Desai puts, "Then, of course there were those who lived and died illegal in America and never saw their families."

Often it is argued that,Post -colonial writing is transcultural in its spirit in the sense that authors are not neatly tide, either culturally or personally to their countries of origin. A sense of origin or belonging is often conspicuously absent. Furthermore, the setting and scope of post-colonial writing is international rather than local in focus. So, often they talk about immigrants' problem and their plight in the other world. If we look at the following extract from the novel **A Bend in River** (1979) by V. S .Naipaul, the narrator, Salim, a man of East African Muslim descent is making observations about the life of immigrants and refugees in London:

> *They traded in the middle of London as they traded in the middle of Africa. The goods traveled a shorter distance but the relationship of the trader to his goods remained the same. In the streets of London I saw these people, who were like myself, as from a distance I saw the young girls selling packets of cigarettes at midnight, seemingly imprisoned in their kiosk, like puppets in a puppet theatre. They were cut off from the life of the great city where they had come to live, and I wondered about the pointlessness of*

> *their own hard life, the pointlessness of their difficult journey.*
> (Barlow:2001,P.10)

The author of this novel was born in Trinidad of Hindu Indian descent, but has lived most of his adult life away from the place of his birth, much of it traveling in Africa and India. So he has the first hand experience of the immigrants' life in a foreign country, as a transcultural writer his writing shows a sense of rootlessness often such writer experience exile. Their writing deals with the search for identity.

In ***The Inheritance of Loss***, we clearly see that there is a constant inward struggle for identity. It is a dark world where the truth seems foggy. The characters are entangled in a state of confusion. The external situation is beyond their control. They often can't comprehend what is happening. This is true in the case of Sai. Sai is a convent bred girl. She speaks English and reads National Geographic. The geographical condition of Kalimpong and problems arising from it are far from her thoughts. The whole movement for homeland and Gyan's support to it are something she cannot understand. Because she belongs to a different society. She cannot identify herself with the situation. Even Gyan, who is an educated youth, feels that his identity is his community, and he must work for it. And perhaps this is the reason why he deserts Sai.

The novel successfully voices the global terrorism. Terrorism has changed the whole scenario of the world. Today we live in constant fear of this. Desai ironically tells us how in the name of homeland some people are terrorizing the innocent. It seems that the new generation has inherited this and the escape from this is almost impossible.

Apart from other major problems discrimination against women folk in general and their exploitation is also presented effectively. The way they have been treated by their counterparts are all described. Mainly it is presented through the character of Nimi -Jemubhai's wife. She belongs to a Patidar Community in Gujarat in which big dowries are taken in marriage. Jemubhai's brutality to his wife is a good specimen of how even the educated people treat a woman. Jemubhai as a servant of British Empire, feels shocked when his is superior inform him about his wife's participation in political events. She was invited to join a procession to welcome Nehru which she had done without knowing its repercussion. Desai writes

> *For the first time he hit her, ... He emptied his glass on her head. Then, when this wasn't enough to assuage his rage, he hammered down with his fists, raising his arms to bring them down on her again and again, rhythmically, until his own hands were exhausted and his shoulders next day were strained sore as if from chopping wood. He even limped a bit, his leg hurting from kicking her. (p. 304)*

The judge's treatment of his wife shows our age old mentality. Though the judge was a well educated person he didn't hesitate while deserting her for no substantial reason. The lady was also humiliated by her uncle when she returned home with the following words:

> *"You are your husband's responsibility... go back your father gave dowry when you married- you got your share and it is not for daughters to come claiming anything thereafter. If you have made your husband angry, go ask for forgiveness." (p. 306)*

Desai shows her awareness of women's exploitation in India. She also highlights their cruel fate in the following words,

> *Oh, this country, people exclaimed, glad to fall into the usual sentences, where human lives are cheap, where standards were shoddy, where stoves were badly made and cheap saris caught fire as easily-" (p. 307)*

This shows how brutal the society is in which we live. Desai tells us all these plainly in her novel.

3.2 Narrative Techniques

In the recent years, the literary world has witnessed a change in the way the narrative is presented in the novel. The modern writers have experimented with the style of writing and they are equally rewarded for that. Both

Arundhati Roy and Kiran Desai are such creative writers. They have made their readers spell bound by their extraordinary narrative techniques. The clever handling of the point of view has showered them with critical acclaim.

Kiran Desai got international acclaim when she won the Booker Prize for her second novel ***The Inheritance of Loss***, which has been described by reviewers as 'the best, sweetest, most delightful novel'. Kiran Desai is highly praised for her literary genius. One of the judges, Hermon Lee, of the Booker Prize commented while announcing the winner,

> *We are delighted to announce that the winner of the Man Booker Prize for 2006 is Kiran Desai's The Inheritance of Loss, a magnificent novel of humane breadth and wisdom, comic tenderness and powerful political acuteness. The winner was chosen, after long, passionate, and generous debate, from a shortlist of five other strong and original voices.*
> *(The Booker press release)*

The novel shuttles between Jemubhai's life and Biju's struggle. At the same time, it has a backward and forward movement in Jemubhai's narrative. The novel offers all the pleasures of traditional narrative in a form and voice that are utterly fresh. Desai's use of the omniscient point of view has the naturalness of some of the finest writer of the English fiction. It is this aspect of her narrative that catches our attention.

The point of view signifies the way a story gets told- the mode (the modes) established by an author by means of which the reader is presented with the characters, dialogue, actions, setting, and events which constitute the narrative in a work of fiction. The question of point of view has always been a practical concern of the novelist. Point of view is one of the most prominent and persistent concerns in modern treatments of the art of prose fiction. There are two basic ways of storytelling: The novelist can tell his story from the inside, that is, he can make one of the characters do it, or he can tell it from the outside as a more or less omniscient author, in a third person point of view or omniscient point of view. Here, the narrator is someone outside the story who refers to all the characters in the story by name, or as *he, she,* and *they.* Kiran Desai introduces Sai in the beginning of the novel in the following words,

> *Sai, sitting on the veranda, was reading an article about giant squid in an old National Geographic. Every now and then she looked up at Kanchenjunga, observed its wizard phosphorescene with a shiver. The judge sat at the far corner with his chess board,, playing against himself.* (P.1)

Desai as a third person narrator tells us al the necessary things about her character. Within this mode, the intrusive narrator is one who not only reports, but also comments on and evaluates the actions and motives of the characters and sometimes express personal views about human life in general as:

> *Could fulfillment ever be felt as deeply as loss? Romantically she decided that love must surely reside in the gap between desire and fulfillment, in the lack, not the contentment. Love was the ache, the anticipation, the retreat everything around it but the emotion itself.* (p.-2)

While writing the novel, the novelist considers the focus of his story, number and relations of his characters, the complexity of his plot and structure, the meaning of his story etc. The ultimate objective of the narration is to achieve verisimilitude. Although first person narration is the more direct method, the third person narration has some objectivity in it. The narrator keeps a safe distance from his characters which gives him freedom to handle his materials.

Kiran Desai's **The Inheritance of Loss** has a wider canvass. It moves to different cultures of the world and travels between two continents. At the same time, the narrative moves between Jemubhai's past when he was a judge- a Sahib and his present condition in the distant town of Kalimpong, where he is living like an outcaste. Biju, on the other side, is struggling in New York to make his living. Both these characters are totally different from each other and the only thing that is common between them is their loss of identity. But Kiran Desai brilliantly portrays them, giving equal weighing to them. And at same time authorial presence is felt. The story is not told 'sequentially', it moves back and forth in time.

Desai begins the novel with the beautiful atmosphere of Kalimpong. This is a chronological presentation of the events which unfold after that in that Himalayan valley. Desai introduces almost all the major characters in this chapter, and at the same time gives us some hint about the upcoming events. She has kept all the strings in her hand and handles them alternatively like a master craftsman. She tells all the minute things about the characters. The Judge, Sai, Gyan, the cook etc. are the characters who are victims of insurgency in the region which drives the novel in the present situation but within this we have private past life of the Judge-Jemubhai which shaped his present life. But it is Biju's narrative that strikes our imagination. Desai tone is ironic here. Like his life, Biju's narrative travels on an uneven path, even though it gives us a pleasant reading experience by avoiding monotony of the traditional plain narrative.

Thus, it is the third person narration which is employed throughout the novel, with an omniscient author narrating the tale from shifting point of view. But we often see authorial comments.

The central events in the novel are insurgency in the valley of the mount Kanchenjunga and the problems of illegal immigrants. The central characters like Jemubhai, Sai, Gyan, the cook, Biju are in one way or other victims of the prevalent condition. Kiran Desai meticulously works among them. She is an omniscient narrator who has all sorts details regarding the characters and the events. She shifts her point of view often and sometimes she herself comments on the situation.

Kiran Desai constantly moves between Biju's story and Jemubhai's story. She has presented their narrative in alternate chapters. Desai simultaneously progresses in both the stories. But as the readers, we see that Biju's story is full of action and events. His job in the various restaurants and his return journey to Kalimpong, all these are eventful. He has been presented like a picaresque hero, who struggles in his journey and learns the ways of the world whereas; the judge's story is more about his past life. Jemubhai's narrative is more or less governed by his reminiscence. Here, Desai explores his personality. The readers are given full detail of Jemubhai's life, from his birth in Piphit – a small village in Gujarat to his journey in England for study and his life as a judge in India. Desai uses a minor character of the cook as the narrator from whose point of view Jemubhai's past life is revealed. But often Jemubhai's is also seen nostalgic.

However, there are several stages of the action of the novel where the chief characters are not present. But the omniscient author is present, and knows, and the authorial voice narrates. Desai often comments no the GNLF movement and its consequences, about which either Biju or Jemubhai are least aware.

In the novel, there are several passages which are devoted to the reflections of the characters. As a matter of fact, Desai shows the inner world of her characters. This is particularly seen in the judge's narrative because he is aloof to external world. He is always alone playing chess with himself brooding about this past life. Desai writes,

> *The judge stared at his chessboard, but after the burning memory of his beginning, he experienced the sweet relief now of recalling his life as a touring official in the civil service.(p.-61)*

We have passages exclusively devoted to Jemubhai's reflection. His childhood experiences, his condition in Cambridge, his life as a judge, his contempt for his wife all are presented with great detail. The old days at Cambridge, especially, haunts Jemubhai because as an Indian he was subject to humiliation in the racist England. It was the most agonizing period of his life. He endured all these only to be like them- a sahib in the Britishraj. Kiran Desai recreates colonial period before the eyes of the readers.

Desai's characters are the victims of the post-modern realities. The international scenario rejects them or they are misfit for it. Desai raises some of the contemporary issues which trouble the whole world and her characters are not exception.
As an omniscient narrator, the novelist keeps the readers well informed by occasionally commenting on the events. Desai shows her strength as

novelist by closely gripping her characters with her unique narrative. She is highly praised for this.

In the novel, kiran desai closely follows the chronological time. Though her main focus is on the life of the judge and Biju but she also given us idea about what is happening in the world at the sometime. Her characters move in time and space, backward and forword . Kiran desai does their time. Kiran Desai does this by presenting various historical events in her course of the narrative. They have impact on the lives of her characters. They sometimes become the victims of there events and sometimes they are silent witness to them.

Kiran Desai tells us about pre-independence India, blood shed during the participation of India-Pakistan and Nehru regime. In the narrative, they all have been presented along with her comments. All her characters are involved with the various historical events which are important from the point of view of our nation building. It also focuses on the past mistake of creating states on the name of race, religion and language which even still cause troubles. Desai puts all with her main stream story to give a touch of realism.

As a writer she shows her immense talent in describing the nature. Her narrative is close with the nature. Some time the moods of her characters and happenings are conveyed by the corresponding changes in the natural elements. In the novel, Kiran Desai's use of mount Kanchenjunga is one of such instance. She uses it to show the condition of her characters. In fact the novel begins with description of Kanchenjunga, evoking a mood of mystery.

The description of mount Kanchenjunga crept in, either intensifying the mood or offering a comment on the events. During the moments of despair Kanchenjunga is presented as follows: "Cloudy peaks of Kanchenjunga" whereas in the end of the novel Biju's meeting with his father is presented as " bright peaks of Kanchenjunga". Desai shows that people of that religion are very much connected with the nature, and she presents nature as living entity. Love, hope, despair, fear, mystery etc. are presented with the description of dark, cloudy, misty peaks of Kanchenjunga. She ends the novel in the following words:

> *The five peaks of Kanchenjunga turned golden with the kind of luminous light that made you feel, if briefly, that truth was apparent. All you needed to do was to reach out and pluck it. (p.324)*

So, one can say that the peaks of Kanchenjunga become a recurrent motif.

Kiran Desai leaves nothing vague , she presents everything vividly. One of the entities presented artistically is the beautiful house of the judge- Cho-Oyu, in the foothill of mount kanchenjunga. The judge purchased it from a Scotsman whose adventurous spirit is felt in the house. It appears as a perfect house for the judge who wants to live a life in isolation. The house is as mysterious as the inmates. Desai's acumen as a writer is seen in its description. No one can deny that it is a perfect house for the person like the judge.

3.3 Art of Characterization

When we read a novel or play for the first time, we are likely to be struck by the story and also by the characters. The characters are the people in the novel. They are very much like the people we meet in our day-to-,day life. In the course of the novel, we might dislike, admire or sympathize them. We form an impression of them by whatever they do or say or feel and sometimes by others opinion about them. But without proper study of these characters, our impression is often one sided. We go by the outward appearance of these characters, and often this thing leads to misinterpretation of the whole personality behind those characters. The study of characters is therefore an important element of the study of any novel. The novel grows by the complexity in the character portrayal and when that complexity of the characters gets revealed, we come to know about progression of the themes.

In *The Inheritance of Loss*, we have two kinds of characters. The first type of characters are the major characters like the judge, Biju, Sai and Gyan, who are directly related to the theme of the novel and who are instrumental in moving the story. The second type is of the minor ones like the cook, Uncle Potty, Father Booty, Noni, Lola, Saeed Saeed etc. are important too, but they are not actively involved in our story. However these characters stand as sharp contrast to our leading characters. Kiran Desai uses them to enhance the effect of her theme. Technically we can divide the characters of the novel as individual and type or representative.

If we go by the definition that characters are the people who live and experience the themes, we clearly narrow it down to our few major characters like Jemubhai the judge Biju, Sai and Gyan. Kiran Desai as an omniscient narrator has given full detail of their life, what they look like, now they speak and dress, their social class, interests and opinions etc. Her two major characters the judge and Biju dominate the novel. The narrative constantly shuttles between their lives. Both of them are, as such, not related each in anyway. So, Kiran Desai keeps two tracks by handling both of them simultaneously. They are the major contributors to our theme. It is their experiences in life which make the major part of the novel. Kiran Desai vividly portrays them. She draws two contradicting personalities. Biju is a restless soul, living almost erratic life, in New York whereas we have the judge who lives far from the madding crowd in the remote Kalimpong. Desai's narrative gives justice to both of them.

The Inheritance of Loss is often called a story of a few powerless people who are struggling for identity. Desai's characters are victims of the situation. The external forces are beyond their control. They don't lead but they are led by the forces. Often they appear as mere puppets in the hands of destiny.

Kiran Desai presents her characters by various modes. She tells us about their external behavior and at the same time we have other characters who impart us necessary details about some particular person. Their thoughts and action are brilliantly portrayed to understand his or her personality as a whole. Desai, in her very first chapter, introduces all her major characters. She also tells us about their nature in just one line. Jemubhai- the judge is introduced to us like this "The judge sat at the far corner with his chessboard, playing against himself". By nature the judge is a very solitary figure. He never entertains any visitors, or we never see him chit chatting whole heartedly with anyone. So, Desai indicates about him in the very first line. The judge is living with his grand- daughter Sai, who is an uninvited guest or a liability for him. He has a cook to look after his day to day needs. The judge has chosen to live in Kalimpong after his retirement. It's a secluded place near the foothill of Kanchenjunga. His only love is his dog Mutt. In that respect, he surprises us. Perhaps his anglophile nature has taught him to love the pet, and hate human beings. He is cold and indifferent to the life around him.

While telling us about the judge's story, Kiran Desai constantly moves between past and present. The judge's present life as a retiree is observed by the omniscient narrator whereas she chooses the judge's cook to tell us about his past life. The cook is a constant companion to the judge from his early days. Sai's arrival in the house and her curiosity to know about her grand-father's life brings to light some facts of the judge's life.

Desai shows the judge as a retiree who is totally engrossed in himself. Sai's first meeting with him, and the impression she forms about him is worth quoting Sai feels, "Oh, Grandfather more lizard than human". Perhaps, various incidents occurred in his life made him so. As a teenage boy, he used to live in Piphit in Gujarat. At the age of twenty, he was sent to Cambridge for I.C.S.. He was married at that time. Jemubhai's departure to England changed his life.

Jemubhai was like an alien in England. He passed through some of the worst experiences of life for being brown in a country of white. We see him as a timid, helpless, tortured figure. Kiran Desai points,

> *He [Jemu] worked twelve hours at a stretch, late into the night and in thus withdrawing, he failed to make a courageous gesture outward at a crucial moment and found, instead that his pusillanimity and his loneliness had found fertile soil. He retreated into a solitude that grew in weight day by day. The solitude became a habit the habit, became the man, and it crushed him into a shadow.* (P.39)

Jemu felt barely human in the racist England. He always felt that he was being observed by those hostile English eyes. And the occasional comments on him, made almost impossible for him to feel comfortable in the country. As it is put,

> *Thus Jemubhai's mind had begun to wrap; he grew stranger to himself than he was to those around him, found his own skin odd coloured, his own accent peculiar. He forgot how to laugh, could barely manage to lift his lips in a smile and if he ever did, he held his hand over his mouth, because he couldn't bear anyone to see his gums, his teeth.* (P.40)

Jemubha's stay in England and his experiences there made him bitter. He suffers from inferiority complex. He felt embarrassing to be Jemubai Popatbhai Patel. So, he changed himself in the English manners.

Perhaps by presenting Jemubhai's past life, Kiran Desai wants to justify what made him indifferent to the world. Back home, Jemubhai is a different person. He has some English tastes and feels ashamed of his wife, who is an uneducated lady. The lady is altogether neglected by him and he leaves her to save his face. Throughout the novel, Desai shows Jemubhai as an identity conscious person. His actions, thoughts, behaviour all are governed by the single cause of identity. That is perhaps the reason why the novel begins with the incident that challenges Jemubhai-the judge's sense of identity. The judge was made to serve tea to the hooligans, was perhaps the most humiliating act for such a man. Kiran Desai writes,

> *Both Sai and the cook had averted their gaze from the judge and his humiliation... It was an awful thing, the downing of a proud man. He might kill the witness.* (P.8)

Jemubhai's aloofness is a result of that lost identity. He cannot adjust in the new situation. He is of brooding nature. Quite often we see him reflecting about the past experiences. His only socializing with old friend Bose proved to be disastrous. He thought Bose was enjoying at his cost. He immediately decided never to meet him again. He cares for position, self respect and dignity.

The judge is never shown worried about anybody except for his beloved pet Mutt. The loss of Mutt is unbearable for him because for Mutt is the only living creature on whom he showers his affection. He almost wept for her.

Desai presents a complex personality through the judge's character. She puts him through the crisis, which shapes his personality. His past experiences have made him bitter. Through his character Desai presents a class of people who are under colonial influence. They had a good time under the Britishraj. They enjoyed their position but the new world order has changed everything. They feel like an alien in this new globalised environment. Their old glory is no more now. And that fact has affected the judge's personality. For the Judge that fall from the grace is unbearable.

Kiran Desai's portrayal of Biju is fascinating. Biju's life is eventful. He is the only son of the judge's cook. He has been sent to New York to make his fortune. The cook is happy with his progress there and like any other father he is fond relating his son's account. But the story is altogether different. Biju's hardship is an eye opener. America lures people like Biju only to be dumped in some poorly ventilated kitchen of their restaurants. Desai ironically tells about the plight of those illegal immigrants. Their struggle for the green card is highlighted through Biju. Kiran Desai while introducing Biju tells us,

> *Biju was his [the cooks] son in America. He worked at Don Pollo or was it The Hot Tomato? Or Ali Baba's Fried Chicken? His father could not remember or understand or pronounce the names, and Biju changed jobs so often like a fugitive on the run-- no papers.* (P.3)

Only in four lines, Kiran Desai tells us everything about Biju. His inconsistent life, his struggle for a good job and the biggest problem that haunts him –'no papers'. He is an illegal immigrant in New York. The word 'fugitive' tells the rest of the story

The Inheritance of Loss presents a post- colonial world which is under the grip of the west. People of the 'third world' see America as land of opportunities. They want be there anyhow, and once they are inside it, they become members of Biju's club contrary to their dreams. Biju is constantly on the run, he cannot work at any place for longer time as he is an illegal immigrant in America. Our first feeling for Biju would be pity. He is a tortured son, disillusioned by the pomp of the west. He considered himself the 'Luckiest boy in the world' when got visa. The picture becomes cleaner when he landed in America. It was the most shocking revelation for him.

It is in Biju's character, that Kiran Desai shows her brilliant art of writing. Desai catches him in various emotions. Though his physical journey is within New York, his mental struggle has universal importance. He wants established himself. He wants his identity in the place where he is living.

Biju is basically an innocent person. People like Saeed Saeed impress him. And Desai often shows contrast between these two persons. Biju is troubled by the circumstances because he has not learnt the ways of the world. He is waiting for the miracle to happen in his life. But as the novel progresses Desai shows us how his dreams are shattered. He realizes that he is not fit for this place. Desai explores the psyche of those illegal immigrants through Biju's portrayal. His journey to Kalimpong and his reunion with father is a moving tale. It seems that finally Desai wants him to breathe some fresh air.

Though, the novel is dominated by the judge and the cook's son Biju, we have also a tender love story of Sai and Gyan against the back drop of insurgency. Desai presents Sai as a typical convent educated girl. She is the grand-daughter of the judge, living with him after her parents' death. She is sixteen years old girl who loves her maths teacher Gyan. Desai has shown her as a sensitive girl. The Judge's cold attitude towards her makes all the more orphan. Through her character Desai shows a typical teenage sensibility. Kiran Desai writes,

> *She sometimes thought herself pretty, but as she began to make a proper investigation, she found it was a changeable thing ,beauty….she transformed her expression from demon to queen. When she brushed her teeth, she noticed her breast jiggle like two jellies being rushed to the table. She lowered her mouth to taste the flesh and found it both firm and yielding.* (P.74)

Kiran Desai's observation of a teenage mind is perfect. Sai has been imparted a spirit that shows her as a girl with self-respect. Her reaction to Gyan's involvement shows her real nature.

Thus, if we analyze Desai's characters, we notice that they represent different classes of the society. It seems that Desai is more concerned with the various issues in the novel. The characters are often overpowered by those issues. Her characters often appear as the victims of the external forces. But still we identify ourselves with people like Biju who dominate the novel. Kiran Desai, at the same time, shows her power of observation through the character of the Judge whose personality is brilliantly revealed. The readers feel the touch of an artist in the portrayal of the characters in the novel.

Kiran Desai through her novel The Inheritance of Loss attempts to address certain global issues that have posed challenges to all developing countries. It is through the mode of irony that Kiran Desai presents the major characters such as Jemubhai, Biju, Gyan and Sai. What strikes the reader as something commendable is her masterly blending of these issues.

CHAPTER - IV
STYLISTIC ANALYSIS OF LANGUAGE

Kiran Desai is one of those Indian English writers who have shown native colours in their writings. She belongs to the group of writers who are global Indians. Their language is English but they are conscious of using it in the Indian style. Though they have native-like proficiency of the English language, they don't want to write in the English way. They have experimented with the language while writing their fiction and tried to represent Indian sensibility. They are no longer imitators of the English writers, but they have their English to tell their tale. They have shown courage in appropriating the English language to suit their purpose and they have been appreciated for it.

Taking inspiration from the post-colonial African writers like Chinua Achebe and Wole Soyinka, the modern Indian English writers have learnt how to use English creatively. The post-colonial writers use the English language as medium of their expression only. They have totally replaced the discourse to suit their style of writing. There are two distinct processes by which they do this: the first, abrogation or denial of the privilege of English, and the second is the appropriation and reconstruction of the language of the empire. The process of capturing and remoulding the language to new usages become important to them.

By *Abrogation* they refuse the imperial standards of using language and by '*Appropriation*' they restructure the English language to suit their culture. As Raja Rao says "to convey in a language that is not one's own, the spirit that is one's own". Thus, they adopt language and utilise it to express their own culture. The English language has that inherent quality to absorb the new elements. As C.D. Narasimhaiaha says (Barlow : 2001), "English is not a pure language but a fascinating combination of tongues welded into a fresh unity." The readers often come across words which are culture specific. Such uses of language as untranslatable words have an important function. They signify a certain cultural experience which they cannot hope to reproduce.

Beginning with Raja Rao, we had many good Indian English fiction writers like G.V. Desani, Salman Rushdie, Upmanyu Chatterjee, Arundhati Roy etc. who have shown the world their English. They experimented with the language and they were highly praised for their new English. These are actually bilingual writers. They use the words phrases, terms from their language in their writings. Their English is the combination the English language and their native culture. They consciously appropriated the English language to carry the impression of their culture.

One of the major features, the post-colonial writing has been its use of English language. The writers have shaped the language to convey their feelings and cultural uniqueness. They feel that they have achieved that status where by they can bring about changes in the language as per their needs. Perhaps the idea behind is that they want to assert themselves. They want to show to the world that they are no longer mere imitator of the English writers. They shaped their English to express themselves.

Though this new English has often confused the native readers, but it has also enriched them. It has emerged as a creative confusion. The writer often uses bilingual terms. We often come across code-switching and code-mixing in their writing. Code-mixing results form linguistic convergence in a bilingual or multilingual setting. Code-mixing contexts are becoming increasingly common in today's world. It is particularly found in urban societies, where people with widely different regional and cultural background live together in close proximity. In India, we often find the mixing of English into Hindi or other regional language discourse. In the words of a renowned sociolinguist B. B. Kachru, 'Code mixing is an outcome of language contact in linguistically pluralistic societies where language dependency might result in developing new, mixed codes of communication'. (1977, p.189) India has been a multilingual country right from the earliest times. Owing to historical reasons, however English bilingualism has become an integral part of Indian consciousness. English bilingualism, however, is quite unevenly distributed in India. The functional use of English vis-à-vis Hindi and other Indian languages varies from state to state and from person to person. Kachru calls it 'a cline of bilingualism'. Such linguistic experiments often give novelty to the narrative. It reduces the monotony of traditional narratives. But it is not always interesting.

Some times the reader may form some misconception about the whole thing or wrongly interpret the text. At the same time it often breaks the link when you don't follow any term used in the native language. Earlier writers often used to give footnotes or glossary of such terms. But it has become out of date now. Recent writers force their readers to stretch their imagination to follow them or consult a good dictionary to follow their terms.

In the Indian English Fiction G.V. Desani, Salman Rushdie and Arundhati Roy can be traced as such writers who made linguistic experiments in their writings. They all are users of the English language as their first language. They have native proficiency in the language. But they all distinctively blend their cultural taste in the English language. Though it had made their text difficult to understand for the readers, nevertheless they are praised for their linguistic creativity. The have almost began new trend in the English fiction. If we closely analyse Kiran Desai's **The Inheritance of Loss,** we will notice that she is a part of that tradition. In her creative use of language, Kiran Desai catches our attention. We can see a close link between her writing and the earlier writers of this tradition. Her command over the language and her acrobatic use of it mesmerizes the readers.

Kiran Desai's **The Inheritance of Loss** is her second novel. Her first novel **Hullabaloo in the Guava Orchard** (1998) is a simple tale of an unemployed youth. It is very much simple and lucid so far as language is concerned. Desai uses typical Indian English of R.K. Narayan for writing this novel. But for her second novel, which almost took eight years to finish, she showed her genius as a writer. She almost penned thirteen hundred pages and edited it to three hundred pages. She wrote and rewrote it before the final draft, and that pain is clearly seen everywhere in the novel. It comes as a sparkling gem after various process of polishing it.

In the novel, Kiran Desai has extensively used the Hindi terms and expressions. It is almost a bilingual novel like Desani's **All about H. Hatterr** (1948) and Rushdie's **Midnight's Children** (1981). For the second novel it was a big gamble which paid. But it is not that she uses it for the sake of using it. She introduces the readers with the persons and the events where such use comes naturally. There are also some typical culture specific terms and expressions which cannot be translated or the translation may sound ridiculous.

Kiran Desai has stretched language to recreate the bizarre world of her novel. It's a rebellious task on her part. Many critics and writers have praised Kiran Desai's attempt of decolonizing English. The English language which R.K. Narayan has described as being "So transparent that it can take on the tint of any country", has acquired much richness and variety through contact with different cultures which have used the language for creative literature. Desai mixes the Hindi terms and expressions with the English to fuse the spirit of her culture in the novel.

The analysis reveals that they have some common features. If we go by its categories, we will realize that why they have been put like that. The translation of those terms would have been less effective or inappropriate to convey the feeling at the some places. There are terms which are culture specific, it is better to retain them as they are to convey the right feeling. There are words which are purely Hindi. Desai often goes for code-switching and code-mixing throughout the novel. Sentences like *'pucca British accent'* are quite abundant. But what is important is the ease with which she puts them in the novel.

We can put these terms in separate categories to get the right impression for its existence in the novel. There are words related to Indian cuisine like:

> *Pakora, khari biscuit, ladoos, parathas, chapatis, atta, srikhand, tikka masala, tandoori grill, navrattan vegetable cury, dal makhani, pappadum khitchri, kheer, jamun mithai, chhang, paan* etc. (pp.90,...)

These words don't have there English equivalents, so they are put as they are. But we also have words which can be translated into English but put in Hindi to create linguistic pun. These words are:

> *Eendoo (egg), kishmish, kaju (dry-fruits), Loki, tind, khaddu, nimboo, ber (vegetables) mia – bibi* etc. (pp.90,140,270,176..)

We have list of words from Indian languages as:

> *nakara, huzoor, hubshi, desi, kookara Raja (rooster), haveli, maharaja, chokra, bania, dhobi, palki, balli, amavas, Gora, goonda, ganja, lathi, dehati, tatti, busti, puja, prasad etc. (pp.56,149…)*

Apart from this, the novel has many typical Indian expressions as:

> *Bar bar karta rehta hai, Hai hai, humara kya hoga, Kamaal hai ,Baap re, Namste, aayiye baethiye, khayiye!, Bhai dekho, aesa hai rasta roko, Phata – phat, Kem chho, Bilkul bekaar, Arre, Biju to sunao kahani, Hota hai, hota hai etc. (pp.50,190…)*

Desai has used a number of words to show relationship between two persons. The English language doesn't specify certain relation but in Indian languages have specific word for all those complex relations. The novel has words like, *kaka, kaki, masa – masi, phoi – phua etc .(p.58)*

Apart from these, there are words like, *pitaji, beta, sasu, didi, babuji, 'baba'* etc. which are deliberately put in the Indian language to show the intensity of feelings and the mode of adoring kith and kin.

The novel has a number of words related clothing / dressing. As there is no English equivalent words for these. They put as they are. We have *dhoti, pallu, kurta, choli, lehnga, salwar, kameez etc.*

But perhaps the most interesting use of Indian terms is the idiomatic expressions and slangs of our language. Desai has used quite a good number of them in the novel. The novel has expressions like *Uloo ka patha, Soour Ka baccha, char sau bees etc.* we have some obscene words like *bhenchoot, sala ,machoot etc.* as well as words with derogatory meaning like *dehati, desi, gonwallah, goonda, gadha, bephkuph etc.*

Apart from this, we often come across code- mixing and code- switching. This is particularly seen in the words related to greetings and eatables. In the novel, Desai uses *respected pitaji, dhanyawad, Shukriya, Thank you, khari biscuit pie, masala – coloured, rice dal etc.* we have Hindi English mix words like *babyji, masterji, dak bunglow, jungli etc.* often we come across sentences like, *looking like a real gow-wallah?, Krishna and the gopis, village belle at the well, 'batao, whats the story?' etc.* Kachru regards code-mixing as an outcome of both language contact and code-switching marks the speaker's attitude towards and relationship with the other participants in the speech act and also their attitude towards him The implications of code mixing in a linguistically heterogeneous society are sociolinguistically and pedagogically important.

If one goes further, one comes across quite a few lines from Hindi movie songs. Desai's characters seem to be fond of Hindi films. We have songs like:

> "Mera Joota hai japani " from the movie Shri 420, then "Bombay se aaya mera dost" from a Hindi movie and "Chaadni Raate, Pyaar Kit Baate" from an old Hindi movie. (pp.53,273)

Though all such things make it a typical Indian novel, it is often elusive for the foreign readers. Only Indian readers can follow some of things as they are from Indian languages. Kiran Desai has not glossed these Indian words and expressions. It seems to be her brave stance. She shows that courage which may cost her readership. But here she follows the foot step of her literary ancestors like Desani, Rushdie and Arundhati Roy. I think it is tendency of all the modern Indian English writers. They have established themselves as a major group in the world of English fiction writers, and they can afford to take such a risk.

The post-colonial writings have this element as a dominating factor. The writers use English only as a medium. Perhaps for a wide readership but they are culturally attached to their roots. They have appropriated the English language to suit their purpose. Kiran Desai uses of the words and allusion from her culture is her way of showing Indianness in the novel. At the same time her characters are not English. They are Indian, living in a small town. So their language has a rustic touch. Perhaps by using such language, Kiran Desai tries to capture the sensibility of those typical Indians.

The novel has abundance of unconventional English. This is particularly seen in the narrative of Biju. Biju is living in New York, so we have typical American dialects in his narrative and like Biju's life in New York; we have unpredictable English to give us a feeling of Biju's struggle. Quite often, we don't find any syntectic structure in his narratives and sometimes it appear in the form of just bundle of words to convey certain feelings as,

> *He [Biju] stood with his head still in the phone booth studded with bits of stiff chewing gum and the usual Fuck shit cock dick pussy love war, swastikas, and hearts shot with arrows mingling in a dense graffiti garden, too sugary too angry too perverse the sick sweet rotting much of the human heart.(p.233)*

Kiran Desai has also produced some finest pieces in language. Some of her sentences instantly catch our attention. At one place she writes,

> *There were concert hall in Europe where the applause rang like a downpour. (p.223)*

While telling us about judge's humiliation she observes

> *It was an awful thing, the downing of a proud man. He might kill the witness .(p.8)*

So, often her language shows her deep understanding of human psyche and her power of observation. Her verbal exuberance is at its peak when she writes:

> *No fruit dies so vile and offensive a death as the banana. .(p.37)*

Being the daughter of the famous Indian English fiction writer Anita Desai, Kiran Desai's attachment with the words and language is natural. She handles the language with ease. Her study in various countries has helped her to know various Englishes. And she has shown her strong acumen by cleverly using it in her novel.

Desai's verbal exuberance is also seen in her delightful language usage. The way she presents her thought attracts us. She shows some interesting combination of words to enchant the readers. She puts, while telling us about Sai's discovery of her adulthood:

> *When she brushed her teeth, she noticed her breast jiggle like two jellies being rushed to table ....The plumpness jiggliness firmness softness, all coupled together...* (P.74)

At one place, the effect of rain is put in alliterative prose like this,

> *Plunk, ping, piddle, drips fell into the pots and pans placed under leaks.*
> (P.322)

> *A woman... without a witness, without a case* (P.307)

Kiran Desai's language impresses us with its novelty and occasional linguistic pun. Her bilingualism makes the novel interesting and worth reading. But her language may confuse the foreign readers with little background about Indian languages. But one must admit that the way she handles English shows her rich repertoire of the language and at the same time her creative genius.

CHAPTER - V
CONCLUSION

Kiran Desai is a new face of Indian Writing in English. With only two novels to her credit, she has shown her genius as a fiction writer. Being a daughter of renowned Indian English Fiction writer – Anita Desai, Kiran Desai's command over the genre is tremendous. Both her novels have earned her critical acclaim and many literary prizes. Her growth as a novelist is exceptionally good. Her first novel **Hullabaloo in the Guava Orchard** (1998) is a simple tale of an unemployed youth who became 'Baba of the tree', preaching sermons to unexpected devotees. The novel is almost written in a comic mode with the touch of irony. But in her second novel **The Inheritance of Loss** (2006), Desai shows her maturity as a novelist.

One can call **The Inheritance of Loss** as Kiran Desai's the most ambitious work as it almost took eight years to finish. She wrote and rewrote the novel. She is such a prolific writer that she almost wrote thirteen thousand pages as her first draft. She then edited and brought it down to three hundred pages (she admits this in one of her interviews to a daily). One can understand the pain taken for writing the novel. But that love's labour has fulfilled all her expectations. The Booker Prize to the novel is a clear verdict of that.

The study reveals that the novel has that substance that can be worthy of our admiration. The Booker committee describes it as "a magnificent novel of humane breadth and wisdom, comic tenderness and powerful political awareness". Kiran Desai captures the post-colonial chaos in the novel. She imparts us the world which engulfed in its various illusions. But she is not preachy, her tone is ironic with occasional touch of humour – though it's a dark humour. The novel is divided between two worlds, and it seems both the worlds have nothing to offer to the powerless people.

The characters, in the novel, struggle for identity. They make us feel that life is long process of establishing one's identity, or the loss of it will lead to the state in which the judge-Jemubhai lives. Desai knows the Indian psyche well and she brilliantly reveals it through the novel. Biju is just a representative of that class of people who are queuing before various embassies to make their fortune in their mythical world. At the same time, GNLF's movement shows how the world is dividing into separate ghettos. We are narrowing our boundaries in the name of race and religion. All these lead to universal anarchy where innocent people get hooked.

Though Kiran Desai has shown her exceptional craft as a novelist, we find some serious drawbacks in the novel which one can not ignore while analyzing the novel. She often seems to be losing her grip over the narrative. As the novel progresses one can see that her threads of narrative get weaken. The novel is filled with various issues and Kiran Desai handles them all at a time. So often the readers get confused in the details given by her. Sometimes the narrative fails to sustain the interest of the readers as well.

Her too much attention to the various contemporary issues make the novel flat. Often it appears as a commentory on the contemporary world than a work of fiction. The novel fails if we judge it from the standards of aesthetic art. Desai got struck with realism and we get bored by the long narrative of pain and suffering. Terrorism, globlization, and illegal immigrants' problems etc. are everywhere in the novel. And often it makes it a pessimistic novel.

Kiran Desai's constant shuttling between Jemubhai's life and Biju's struggle makes the novel their biographies than a work of fiction. Their detailed stories do not attract the reader's attention. Apart from these, the end of the novel does not convince the readers. Gyan's sudden change surprises the readers also.

Gyan, who was ready to sacrifice himself for the cause, suddenly appears as a changed person. Kiran Desai leaves it to the readers to follow, and the readers are often confused about the sudden change. Before one can understand anything, the novel ends. The end appears as a sudden chain pulling to stop it in a hurry. Kiran Desai seems to have lost her way and does not know where to end the story. So it appears as a haphazard end. Many question remained unanswered in the novel.

Apart from this, Kiran Desai's style of writing the novel has also won her critical applause. She chooses a very unusual method of story telling. Earlier writers like Salman Rushdie and Arundhati Roy seem to have inspired her a lot. One can establish a close link between her writings and her predecessors. Her novel reminds us of Arundhati Roy's **The God of Small Things** (1997) which has a similar narrative. Though **The Inheritance of Loss** in its vastness of theme differs from it, the novel is like an authentic document on the effect of globalization. Kiran Desai seems to have bitter tongue for this new world order. The Americanization of the world is subtly reflected in the novel. The demand for Gorkhaland for the Gorkhas in her novel shows her political awareness. I think she actually wants to show how the innocent people get crushed in such movements. All her characters, in one way or other, are victims of this so called 'freedom struggle' or 'Liberation movement'. She seems to ask To whom all these movements liberates?'

Looking from the linguistic point of view, one notices that the novel is not an isolated piece in the Indian English fiction. It has invisible link with the early masters of Indian English fiction like Raja Rao, G.V.Desani, Salman Rushdie and Arundhati Roy. Their linguistic experiments make them member of a group. These are the writers who have strong sense for their cultural heritage and they have fused their culture in their writings. They have changed the language to suit their purpose and extensively used words and phrases from Indian Languages. Kiran Desai uses number of words and expressions from the Hindi. But she hasn't glossed them anywhere in the novel. It's a clear signal from her as an Indian English writer that now we have attained that position in the realm English fiction that we can experiment with form and language. Her bilingualism, on the contrary, makes the novel all the more fascinating. The novel in its bilingual aspect shows our changing attitudes towards the use of English.

The Booker Prize to **The Inheritance of Loss** is an acknowledgement that the novel fulfills all the criteria of a perfect work of art. And at the same time, it also reveals that the English language is not for any particular nation or race. It is open to new changes and novel elements of other languages of the world. It only needs a good craftsman to handle it creatively. In the case of Kiran Desai, one feels that she has proved that she has that artistry that can leave its mark on the English Literature. The analysis of the novel reveals that she is not just writing words, she has poured her soul into her work like a true artist. Her sincerity in writing is worthy of our praise and admiration.

BIBLIOGRAPHY

Abram, M.H. (1993). *A Glossary of Literary Terms*. Bangalore : Prism Books.

Ashcroft, Bill., Gareth Griffiths. & Heien Tiffins. (1995). *The Post- colonial studies reader*. New York : Routledge.

Barlow, Adrian ed. (2001). *Post- Colonial Literature*. Cambridge University Press.

Das, Bjiaykumar. ed. (2001). *Critical Essays on the Post- Colonial Literature*. New Delhi: Atlanta Pub.

Desai, Kiran (2006). *The Inheritance of Loss*. New Delhi: Penguin Books India.

----------- (1998). *Hullabaloo in the Guava Orchard*. Delhi: Viking India.

Desani, G.V.(1970). *All About H. Hatterr*. New Delhi: Penguin Books India.

Derett, M.E. (1966). *The Modern Indian Novel in English: A Comparative Approach*. University Liber de Bruxelles.

Devy, G. N. (1993). *In Another Tongue : Essays on Indian English Literature*. New Delhi : Creative Books.

Dhawan, R.K. ed.(1994). *Indian Literature Today*. New Delhi: Prestige Books.
Dodiya, J. K. ed.(1999). *Indian Women Writers – A Critical Perspective*. New Delhi : Sarup Sons.

------------.ed.(1999). *The Critical Studies of Arundhati Roy's The God of Small Things*. New Delhi : Sarup Sons.

Gandhi, Leela (2000). *Post- Colonial Theory: A Critical Introduction*. New Delhi : Oxford University Press.

Hawthorn, Jeremy (1998). *A Glossary of Contemporary Literary Theory*. Arnold.

Iyengar, K. R. S. (1985). *Indian Writing in English*, New Delhi : Sterling Publication.

Kachru, B. B. (1981) " The Pragmatic of Non-native Varities of English ." in *English for Cross-cultural Communication* Ed. by Smith,L.E. , London: Mac Millan.

Kachru, B. B. (1977) "Towards Structuring Code-mixing : An Indian Perspective". London: Mac Millan.

Khair, Tabish. Ed.(2003). *Amitav Ghosh : A Critical Companion.* Delhi: Permanent Black.

Khair, I. (2000). *Babu Fiction: Alienation in Contemporary Indian Novel.* New Delhi: Atlanta Pub.

Lodge, David (1993). *The Art of Fiction.* New York: Viking.

Marsh, Nicholas (2002). *How to Begin Studying English Literature.* New York: Palgrave.

Mehrotra, A. K. ed. (2003). *An Illustrated History of Indian English Literature.* New Delhi: Permanent Black.

Mehta, P. P. (1978). *Indo- Anglian Fiction: An Assessment.* Bareily: Prakash Book.

Mukherjee, Meenakshi. (1971) *The Twice Born Fiction* . New Delhi: Arnold Heinemann.

Mukherjee, Meenakshi. (1996) *Realism and Reality: The novel and Society in India.* New Delhi: Oxford University Press.

Pandey, Miti. (2003). *Feminism in Contemporary British and Indian Fiction.* New Delhi : Samp and Sons.

Pathak R.S. ed. (1994). *Recent Indian Fiction.* New Delhi : Prestige Books.

Rajan, P. K. ed. (1995). *Changing Traditions in Indian English Literature.* New Delhi : Creative Books

Roy, Arundhati (1997). *The God of Small Things.* New Delhi : India Ink

Rushdie, Salman (1981). *Midnight's Children*   London: Penguin

Rushdie, Salman and Elizabeth West eds.(1997) *The Vintage Book of Indian Writing in English* . London : Vintage.

Shirwadkar, Meena (1979). *Images of Indo - Anglian Fiction.*   New Delhi : Sterling Pub.

Sureshkumar, A.V. ed. (1996). *Six Indian Novelists.* New Delhi : Creative Books.

Trivedi, Harish. (1999). *"Salman the Funtoosh : Magic Bilingualism in Midnight's Children"* in *Rushdie's Midnight's Children: A Book of Readings.* Ed. by Mukherjee, Meenakshi. Delhi: Pencraft International.

Printed in Great Britain
by Amazon